1001 Ways To Save Money

1001 Ways To Save Money

Quit Flushing Your Hard-Earned Money Down the Toilet

Annie Margarita Yang

Annie Margarita Yang Inc.

Boston, MA

Annie Margarita Yang Inc.
P.O. Box 505149 Chelsea, MA 02150-5149
www.AnnieMargaritaYang.com
Hello@AnnieMargaritaYang.com

Hardcover ISBN: 978-1-961039-05-6
Paperback ISBN: 978-1-548254-59-9
eBook ISBN: 978-1-961039-04-9
Audiobook ISBN: 978-1-961039-06-3

Editing by Barbara Gurgel
Interior Design by Annie Margarita Yang
Book Cover Design by Annie Margarita Yang

This is for you, JP Rodriguez.

Contents

Acknowledgements..3

Preface 5

Introduction..9

1. Basic Money Management...19

2. Savvy Shopping...31

3. Career and Work...43

4. Housing..49

5. Utilities..61

6. Food..79

7. Clothing...101

8. Transportation..121

9. Health and Medical..127

10. Insurance...145

11. Babies and Children 153

12. Toiletries..159

13. Cosmetics and Hair Care 165

14. Cleaning Supplies...171

15. Education and Tuition..173

16. Books..181

17. Office Supplies...183

18. Subscriptions 187

19. Gifts and Holidays...191

20. Furniture 195

21. Love and Relationships..197

22. Pets 205

23. Music and Technology 209

24. Entertainment 219

25. Travel 243

26. Debt 253

Bibliography 259

Share Your Thoughts: Leave a Review 263

About The Author 265

Also By The Author 267

*Too many people spend money they earned..
to buy things they don't want..
to impress people that they don't like.*

—*Will Rogers*

Acknowledgements

I would like to thank my husband, Handrio Nurhan, for providing me the emotional support and encouragement that I needed to complete this project. My experiences and time with Handrio also inspired me to think of many of the creative ways to save money found in this book. Above all, I would like to thank my parents, Ai Kui Yao and Han Jie Yang, for providing financial support while writing this book. Without them, this book would not come to fruition.

I would like to express my profound gratitude to Monique Ar-rucci, Tippy Felzenstein, Robert Guddahl, Rie Iwamoto, Brian Rapsey, and Bobby Soohoo for offering comments and assisting in editing the first edition. Thank you to Barbara Gurgel for editing the second edition.

Preface

How can I save money? This is the first and the most common question that people ask me when I reveal that I teach personal finance. It sounds like a simple question with a simple answer. The answer is this: just do not spend your money. It seems obvious to me.

However, after a religious service meeting one day, my friends Vandana, Jeanette, SoJin, and Samir and I went to a restaurant to eat dinner. Over dinner, Vandana asked me the same old question: "How can I save money?" I suddenly realized that this simple question had a loaded answer. People have different income levels and spending habits so it is difficult for me to provide tips that will truly work in their situation, especially when people can be so secretive about their finances. In Vandana's case, it was my first time ever meeting her, through that religious gathering in her home. She worked in Staten Island and lived in a one-bedroom apartment in Brooklyn. Who was I to tell someone I just met to save money by renting a studio in Staten Island instead to 1) decrease the square footage she occupied while still maintaining privacy and 2) live in Staten Island to save money on gas and/or bus fare and forget about convenient access to hip restaurants in Brooklyn? And by the way, don't waste money on decorating your apartment either until you own your own house. My advice works, but I didn't feel comfortable saying that, and she probably wasn't going to take my advice anyway! But on the flip side, telling her the classic generic advice, spend less than you make, wouldn't do her any good either. I knew plenty of ways to save money—too many to count, in fact! Thus, I felt inspired to answer that question to the best of my ability and create a reference book people can use to pick and choose the tips they did feel comfortable implementing into their lives and doing it at their own pace without feeling like I was judging them for their lifestyle choices or like they were sacrificing the aspects of life they enjoyed the most. The next day, the idea to write this book, *1,001 Ways to Save Money*, was born.

I love saving money. Anyone who knows me well knows that I get a kick out of saving money. I began my journey when I was 18 years old. Fresh out of high school, I had a dream to forgo college and carve my own path in life. I wanted to travel the world, and the only way to accomplish that was to start working and saving money for my adventure. I always saved at least 25 percent of my income. At one point, I saved 50 percent. Saving became second nature for me. After two years of working full-time as a cashier who wore multiple hats, my bank account balance was $13,000.00. Not bad for a 20-year-old. I did enroll in college eventually and completed both an associate degree and a bachelor's degree in communications.

My colleagues wondered how I managed to save so much while they struggled living paycheck to paycheck. It was hard to explain my lifestyle or how I did what I did. Writing this book challenged me to think deeply about my process so I could teach others to live likewise. At times, I doubted my knowledge and my experience, but I realized I know more than I think. Also, the message is more important than the messenger. I had to let go of my fears, as many people desperately need the information I am offering. Too many people who work hard to make their money never seem to be able to get ahead financially. You work too hard for your money to have nothing to show for it in the end.

One colleague who inspired me and propelled me to write this book was JP Rodriguez. I met JP while working at the Overton Hotel as a banquet server. He was the banquet captain, and he was one of the few people who cared about how working at the hotel interfered with my personal life. Management expected everyone in the banquets department to consistently work 70 to 80 hours a week, which was outright insane. The pay was good, but the job was almost like slave labor. We were given start times for our shifts but no end times. Everyone working in banquets was only allowed to leave when all the work was finished... whenever that was.

JP was the only person there who took me aside on my first day on the job and was frank with me about how working such long hours could ruin my life outside of work. His own marriage was in trouble—his wife and daughter never saw him much and wondered when he would be coming home. Sadly, he had bills to pay and a family to support just like most people I met, so he was stuck at his job. He couldn't afford to leave because during the last time he was unemployed, he applied around for five months before finally getting this one. I was so saddened to hear his story that by the time I got home, I couldn't help but cry uncontrollably. His story inspired me to finish this book. I was halfway through writing this book at the time, and then I thought of all 1,001 ways to save money by the next evening.

Ideally, no one should be in a situation like JP's. However, through my experience, I have found that unless you live in absolute poverty, you play a role in creating this kind of situation, and you can get yourself out of it. Take control. You are the driver, not the passenger, in your life. You can steer yourself in a different direction if you so choose. Your life is not anyone else's responsibility but your own. If you are in a situation where you work hard but somehow never have any money left at the end of the month, this book is perfect for you.

Chapter 1

Introduction

I am the daughter of Chinese immigrants, born and raised in America, caught between two cultures. My parents were young children at the start of China's Cultural Revolution in 1966.

My mother was born in rural China to farmers. They lived without running water, drawing from a nearby well instead. In the 1960s, widespread famines and shortages caused food rationing, especially gain. To obtain food, you needed both money and a food ration coupon. When necessary, rice grains were used to make congee to feed everyone in the family. Congee is the symbol of poverty and hardship. This poor man's meal is made from slow cooking a ratio of one cup rice to 10 cups water.

Meat was a luxury back then, so my mom's side of the family saved and accumulated meat coupons and redeemed them for special occasions like Chinese New Year and birthdays. Even then, meat was chopped into small pieces and used to add flavor to vegetable dishes, not served individually like steaks.

My mom often dreamt of stumbling upon a box of cookies and hiding them under her pillow to save for later. She would wake up and realize it was all a dream. She dropped out of school in 6th grade to work hard labor jobs to help support her family.

My dad grew up in the city. He rarely spoke much about his childhood, so the only thing I can tell you is that he was extremely smart. He finished valedictorian in the high school's graduating class of 1977 and then went on to college. Hearing this story growing up, I always thought it was no big deal since college is a big business in America and will practically take anybody. Here in America, it's not a question of whether you will get into college. It's a question of how much prestige the college has and whether you can afford it. I didn't truly understand the historical context and its significance of my dad's college acceptance until this year.

To enter college in China, applicants need to take a national university entrance exam. In 1966, the Chinese abolished the exam, condemning it elitist. University students already in college when this went into effect had their studies suspended. No one in the entire country was allowed to go to college, until the government resumed the national university entrance exam in August 1977. That year, competition was fierce, as a decade's worth of high school graduates, along with those who had their studies halted in 1966, competed for a university spot, in addition to that year's graduating high school class. Only five percent of examinees qualified to enter university. My dad was the only one from his entire school who went to college.

When immigrants arrive in the United States seeking the American dream, they aren't seeking the white picket fence. They are seeking equality of opportunity and the right to life, liberty, and the pursuit of happiness. Imagine growing up in a country where no amount of money could buy food and no one in the entire country could get a college education. All my parents wanted was an opportunity to make a better life for themselves. My dad arrived here first, with a few hundred dollars in his pocket. My mom arrived three years later. My dad was so poor, he couldn't afford a taxi to the airport. He was late picking her up because he had to take the bus to get there and then take the bus back home together. That was the only moment in my mom's entire life he gifted her fresh flowers and he never did it again because flowers are a waste of money.

I grew up poor. I wore hand-me-down clothes from my brother until I felt way too embarrassed to dress like a boy. I always shared my bedroom with a sibling. At some point in my childhood, there were six of us sharing one bathroom. Heat and hot water were included in our rent, so our landlord would set the heat to the legal minimum of 62 degrees Fahrenheit at night. I walked around the apartment with my puffy down jacket on and my hands and feet were constantly freezing. In the summers, we used a portable air conditioner to keep cool, but it would fill up with water every 3 hours. I never got a good night's sleep in the summers because I got up twice per night to empty the water tank. My parents never took us to a restaurant unless it was for a special occasion. At 14 years old, I got a boyfriend, and he took me to Cold Stone Creamery. I was totally clueless on how to order ice cream. I felt so embarrassed because all my friends seemed to intuitively know how to order food at a restaurant and not me.

We were poor, but we definitely did not live in poverty. Rent and utilities were always paid on time. There was always food on the table. We had running water and a refrigerator and microwave—things my mom never had growing up. I always had clothes to wear and new shoes when my feet outgrew the old ones. My parents were outrageously frugal and spent only on necessities but spent big on things they thought were super important. When it came to my health, my mom always bought me designer prescription glasses and used the best orthodontist she could find for my braces even though he didn't take our dental insurance. When it came to education, they refused to pay for standardized test prep (in their eyes, that was not an education). However, they did pay for private guitar and singing lessons.

They saved and contributed $7,500 into a 529 college savings account for me. In ten years, the investments doubled to $15,000. I went to community college for free and then used $10,000 for my entire bachelor's degree. Since I could not use the remaining $5,000 on nonqualified education expenses without incurring a tax penalty and I had zero plans on continuing my formal education, I transferred all of it to my husband's name. $5,000 was enough to pay for my husband's entire master's degree tuition.

Because of my parents' background and my upbringing, I had a hard time comprehending why people in the United States complain so much about how hard it is to save money. Working full-time earning a minimum wage, renting a room in a four-bedroom apartment with roommates, I felt freaking rich. For once, I had my own privacy and the walls were thick enough to not hear the kitchen faucet running when my bedroom door was closed. There was gorgeous Italian ceramic floor tile throughout the apartment, compared to the tile I had growing up that looked gross no matter how much I mopped it. The flood lights on my bedroom ceiling made me feel like I was living in a hotel. On minimum wage full-time, I saved 25% of my income, paid rent and all bills on time, and spent the rest on whatever I wanted. Even with all the raises I've gotten throughout the years, I've continued following the same formula.

Here's the difference though: saving 25% of my income from my very first job meant I wasn't able to enjoy many of the comforts that other people seemed to have. I was definitely uptight with making sure I always stayed within my budget no matter what. It wasn't until after I bought my first home, feeling like I finally overcame a financial milestone many in their 20s can't even fathom achieving without parental help, that I finally let myself relax and spend a bit more money for comfort. Before buying my first home, I never bought a microwave, toaster oven, bathroom scale, TV, sofa, nightstands, or any of the things that were considered normal things to own. I considered these things luxuries, not necessities, so I did without. When I had to break my lease to move into my new home, prospective subletters looked at my living room which fit only two office desks for me and my husband to work at home, and wondered how we got by without a TV and sofa. My husband and I worked our butts off to work and earn more money and the furniture in our home reflected our priorities.

Is the American dream dead? I believe in the United States, there is an abundance of opportunities and money to go around. No, we are not all given the same opportunities, but we all have an opportunity to study, earn, save, and invest. It's not fair to graduate college with student loan debt and then find that the entry-level jobs pay a pittance, while someone else was born into a well-off family with connections that land them a cushy job from the get-go. But if that is the opportunity you've been handed, make the most of it.

I actually think starting from the bottom is a great situation to be in. You have nowhere to go but up! When you start with low pay and live on a budget while saving a minimum 10% of your income, it can motivate you to do better. You may develop an unstoppable hunger that can't be matched. In a real estate company that I worked at, the owners constantly complained that they couldn't seem to motivate the poorer-performing agents to close more deals. To motivate those agents, they offered cash bonuses for hitting certain targets, but it never worked. The top-performing agents always got the bonuses because they were self-motivated.

Low-paying jobs usually pay hourly so you make sure to show up on time and get paid every dollar you can. You might even work more than 40 hours/week or work multiple jobs to make ends meet. The schedules change weekly, making it difficult to plan ahead. These jobs usually force you to be on your feet all day even when it's not busy. There's also usually no designated lunch break where you can actually sit down and eat in peace. These jobs suck, but every day is a new day to practice doing the work with a smile on your face. Attitude makes all the difference.

With each new job, your skills command more money and you can save 50% and spend 50% of every raise. You gain the kind of confidence that can never be taken away from you because you know nothing was handed to you. When you get to this point in your life, you appreciate all the comforts that your colleagues take for granted because you know what it's like to start from the bottom. You'll also look at your future colleagues and wonder why they complain about their well-paying jobs with good benefits so much, somehow always show up late for everything and get away with it, get tired so easily when they sit at a desk all day, and last but not least, wonder why they always live paycheck to paycheck.

The simple answer to that last one is debt. The average American household owed $137,729.00 in debt in 2019. Nationally, Americans owe a combined $14.3 trillion in debt. For 80 percent of Americans, debt is a way of life. For 76 percent of Americans, living paycheck to paycheck is the norm. Half of Americans say that they would not be able to come up with $1,000.00 to pay for an emergency (Ostroski, 2021). They use credit cards and home equity loans when emergencies happen. This is no laughing matter. I have come across many people who think that it is okay to have debt and that they can take their time paying it off. I disagree. I am completely against debt unless it is used as an investment tool to make more money.

Debt is one of the biggest obstacles to accumulating wealth. It sucks away your income, which is your most powerful wealth-building tool, one dollar at a time. It is the result of a combination of overspending, which is within our control, and medical debt, which is more difficult to have control over in the United States due to astronomical health care costs. More important than how much you make is how much you save. There are plenty of people who make a lot of money but also spend a lot of money. They never get ahead financially because they never save.

Think of people who hit the lottery jackpot or receive a large inheritance. Many of them end up broke in just a few years. When lottery winners received half their prize, they saved only 16% of it (Imbens, Rubin, & Sacerdote, 2001). The Certified Financial Planner Board of Standards says nearly a third of lottery winners declare bankruptcy (Edelman, 2016). Why? They squander the money away on houses, cars, vacations, gifts, and other ridiculously expensive things. They never lived below their means when they were poor, so when they became rich, they continued doing the same thing and eventually lost it all. Money is easy to make but hard to keep.

Self-made millionaires who were interviewed in Thomas Stanley and William Danko's book, *The Millionaire Next Door*, all saved and invested 20 percent of their income. They did not save because they were rich. They became rich because they saved. They led a modest life, not a life of glamor. The typical self-made millionaire was self-employed, received no inheritance, lived in a lower middle-class neighborhood, drove an older model car, and wore inexpensive suits. Funnily enough, first-generation millionaires amassed their wealth because they understood the value of saving money. However, their descendants tended to squander that wealth. It takes only 19 days for an average inheritance recipient to buy a new car, and seventy percent of wealthy families lost their fortune within two generations (Taylor, 2015) because they were one step removed from the work ethic and diligence required to make and save money.

What does this have to do with you? You might not become a millionaire, but you can definitely improve your financial situation regardless of the state you are in now. You can think about your own consumer behavior and reflect on how your spending habits have created problems in your life. I believe one of the biggest factors to saving money is to ignore what the people around you are doing. Be weird, be different, and be confident about it too. Too often, I see photos of my high school classmates on Facebook, and I wonder how they can afford their high-consumption lifestyle. I find that my peers never wear the same clothes twice. They travel to foreign countries during spring break every year. They eat at nice restaurants at least once a week. They party and buy alcohol like no tomorrow. They create the impression of having a perfect life on Instagram. Believe me, I do get jealous at times and feel a tinge of FOMO. I often wonder about where they get all their money. I doubt they worked for all of it since they just graduated college and entered the workforce. The answer is, "all flash, no cash," or, "big hat, no cattle." In other words, it is all a façade. They are more likely burdened by student loan debt than anything else. A former classmate I saw on Facebook with the lifestyle I described reached out to me on Facebook for help with her finances. She revealed she had $20,000 in credit card debt. People only show their best moments online for the world to see. As for older folks, everything is most likely financed too. Do not get caught up in the game of keeping up with the Joneses. This sort of lifestyle is unsustainable in the long run. Focus on building your wealth instead.

The Ten Commandments of Saving Money

All the ways to save money in this book are based on 10 principles that I call the Ten Commandments of Saving Money. These principles can be applied in just about any situation: housing, utilities, food, clothing, transportation, medical and health, insurance, recreation, vacation, debt, and much more. You name it, and I've got it in this book. If there is anything you will want to remember after reading this book, this is it:

1. Make saving money your priority.
2. Be content with who you are and what you have.
3. Do it yourself in lieu of paying for convenience.
4. Find free and cheap alternatives.
5. Use less of something or simply make do without.
6. Reuse, maintain, repair, and repurpose your possessions before buying anything new.
7. Research prices, discounts, and reviews before purchasing any products or services.
8. Borrow from or share with others.
9. Say no to people and businesses that want your money but do not act in your best interest.
10. Avoid debt at all costs and pay off your current debts as fast as possible.

Every single way of saving money has been tried and true. Since the only criterion is that it saves money, some of the ways listed are hilarious, while others are downright disgusting enough to make you feel uncomfortable. Everything in this book works. It is up to you to decide which ways to follow.

Saving money has been known to be boring, but try changing your mindset about saving. Personal finance is not boring. It is empowering when you have enough interest and curiosity to learn. In this book, I have kept most of my examples entertaining, humorous, and lighthearted, but I am serious when I need to be. I do this to help you think about saving money from a different perspective. You might get excited when you find out that you can easily save $1,000.00 per year just by reasonably changing one aspect of your lifestyle. You might get excited to know that you can afford that dream vacation you always wanted by cutting back in another spending area. Find what motivates you.

A lot of people believe that saving money leads to being deprived of any pleasure. This couldn't be further from the truth. In order to save money, you need to define what is important to you. After determining your priorities, you align your spending with those priorities while cutting back on the things that do not matter. You derive more joy and contentment from every transaction when you do this. Also, you gain peace of mind knowing what you can and cannot afford right now. In the future, when you have more money saved up, you can afford greater pleasures that you could never afford before.

I understand saving money is a challenge to people who are just starting. This is because it requires behavioral change, and it takes time to form new habits. Instead of trying to change every aspect of your lifestyle at once, pick only one way to save money and then go from there. Change is easier when it is slow. After you adjust to the change, start the cycle over again by picking another way to save money. The most important part is that you do it, and you do it consistently. Any amount of money saved over a long period of time adds up to a large sum. The road to building wealth is a marathon, and slow and steady wins the race.

Chapter 2

Basic Money Management

1. Apply the tips in this book. You will not save any money if you read this book without applying any of the concepts in real life. Back in high school, I had to take a biology lab with Dr. Stephanie Tzall. My group was too lazy to do the experiment, as we already knew what the results would be. We filled in the lab paperwork and called it a day. Dr. Tzall caught on and asked, "Would you rather learn about a country by reading a travel book, or would you rather travel there and experience it yourself?" I cheekily replied that I would rather read a travel book. Dr. Tzall was right, though. The same concept that she used applies to saving money. Reading this book is not enough—you need to act.

2. Pay yourself first. When I taught personal finance to high school students and asked the class what they thought it meant to pay yourself first, one student said, "It means to treat yourself first. For instance, before paying the bills, get yourself a manicure because you need it." I thought her response was hilarious, but unfortunately, her answer was wrong. Paying yourself first means that the first thing you do with your paycheck is to set some aside for your savings. Save between 10 to 15 percent of every dollar you receive. Some people go as far as saving 50 percent of their income. I applaud them. At one point when I lived with my parents and made $1,000.00 per month, I saved 50 percent. However, when I moved out and made $1,600.00 per month, I saved 25 percent. I wished I could have saved more, but I had to pay rent. Still, 25 percent is more than what most Americans set aside.

3. Create and follow a budget. I love budgeting because it lets me know what I can and cannot afford. Budgets also help me align my spending with the things that are important to me. For instance, I love books and travel, so I spend most of my money on those two things. I do not think clothes are a priority, so I spend less on clothes. Stop wasting your hard-earned money on random things you do not care about.

4. Make 28-day budgets. The 28-day budget works particularly well when you get paid every week or every two weeks. It does not work well for people who get paid on the first of every month. With the 28-day budget, you end up creating 13 budgets every year instead of 12. Since you pay rent and utilities 12 times per year, the rent and utility expenses in the 13th budget could go toward something else. I did this one year, and it felt like getting free money when I reached the 13th budget. I saved $650.00 that month in addition to the $400.00 I normally saved every month.

5. Track your expenses. You cannot create an accurate budget without tracking your expenses. You also cannot save money without knowing where your money is going. There are other benefits to tracking money that you might not have ever thought about. For one, you become more mindful every time you shop, which means you might think twice before buying something. Second, it is a great way to see whether your bank statements match your own records. If something is off, a company might have overcharged you or charged you twice. Call and get your money back. Some people become victims of fraud because they never reconcile their bank statements. Third, some companies need proof when handling disputes, which makes accurate record-keeping extremely important. I once needed to cancel my prepaid phone plan with H2O Mobile. I threw out my broken iPhone, accidentally leaving the SIM card inside. The customer service representative wanted me to prove that I was Annie Yang by sending me a text message. I told them it wouldn't work because I just threw out my iPhone along with the SIM card into the dumpster. So, then they asked me when I first activated the account and how much money I paid for my last phone bill. Thanks to my accurate record keeping, I was able to tell them. Keep the tracking process as simple as possible. Keep your receipts throughout the day, and then write down your transactions into a memo book at the end of the day. For digitally savvy people, use an Excel spreadsheet. Write the date, the item, and the amount of money spent.

6. Open a checking account. Five percent of households in the United States do not have a checking account. Without a checking account, you must pay fees to cash your paychecks at a check-cashing place. You should not have to pay money just to access your own money.

7. Open a savings account. Stop burying your cash under your mattress. All your money could be gone in the event of fire, flood, theft, or loss. Another reason to open a savings account is that you should not be keeping all your money in your checking account. Keeping all your money in your checking account makes it harder to track the amount you are saving. It is easy to promise yourself not to spend the $1,000.00 left in your checking account, but very easy to blow through it when you get the urge to spend. Your money should be separated.

8. Set up an automatic transfer from checking to savings. To make it easy for you to save, set up an automatic transfer from your checking account to your savings account. Schedule the transfer to go through on the day after you receive your paycheck, as sometimes you might receive your money late. You never need to think about it, and you end up spending only the remaining amount in your checking account. This method works well for people who have steady paychecks.

9. Save all your coins in a glass jar. I use glass because I like the visual reminder of how much I've saved. I store my coins in a quart-sized Mason jar and then when it is almost full, I roll them up and deposit it into my savings account at the bank. Usually, I have around $50.00 worth of coins. I feel like I'm getting free money every time I count them up.

10. Do the 52-week money challenge. On the first week, save $1.00. On the second week, save $2.00. On the third week save $3.00. Keep adding a dollar for each week. This is like a savings snowball. The snowball gets bigger each week. By the time you reach the 52nd week, you'll have saved $1,378.00. To make this more challenging, do it in higher increments. Some people complete this challenge in increments of $5.00.

11. Do not borrow payday loans. The interest rates are too high, and the interest also compounds daily, which means you owe more than if it were to compound monthly. Ensure that you will always have enough money to last until your next payday by having an emergency fund and by following a budget.

12. Manage your time effectively. Stay organized. Know when all your bills and subscriptions are due and make sure you have enough money in your checking account to pay for them. That way, you never pay another overdraft fee or late fee ever again. You can always call your bank and ask nicely to waive the overdraft fees. Some banks say yes. I never had a problem managing due dates, but I did accidentally overdraft my account one time. I deposited a check at the counter and withdrew cash (less than the amount of that check but more than the amount I had in the bank) in the same transaction. I was young and didn't understand that checks took 23 business days to clear so when withdrawing cash in the same transaction, the cash actually comes from your bank balance and NOT from the check. Lo and behold, I overdrew and got hit with a $35 fee. I called twice and asked nicely for them to waive the fee since it was my first time, and the teller could have told me right then and there that I was going to overdraft instead of letting the transaction go through. Unfortunately, the bank said no. Not all banks will do it, so don't always rely on calling to waive the fees after the fact.

13. Pay off your entire debt balance if you have the savings to do it. People who have enough savings while owing debt can do this. For instance, my friend Brian had $30,000.00 in savings but owed $10,000.00 in student loans. I recommended Brian to pay off his student loans entirely. Brian would still have $20,000.00 remaining in savings. Brian refused and wanted to keep making minimum payments for the rest of his loan term. However, he would be flushing his hard-earned money down the toilet, as he would pay more in compound interest.

14. Consider opening a club savings account. A club savings account is a short-term savings account used to save up for the holidays. Account owners deposit money throughout the year, and the money cannot be withdrawn until the holiday season, which is around October or November. When I was first learning how to save money at 18 years old, I opened a club savings account at my local community bank. I loved it because I made deposits every single week, but I was never allowed to withdraw my money. I opened my account in July, and by October I had saved up $1,000.00. It was during this period of my life that I cultivated the discipline of saving without ever touching my emergency fund.

15. Save 50 percent of every raise and bonus. If you were already living with an annual income of $30,000.00 and doing just fine, the chances are high that you can feel quite satisfied by continuing to live on that amount. Most people fall into the trap of lifestyle inflation, which means they increase their spending when their income increases. In other words, income goes up, and bills go up with it. The things that were once deemed luxuries for young adults turned into necessary comforts for older adults.

There is an easy way to prevent lifestyle inflation. Whenever you get a raise or a bonus or even get a new job with higher pay, save half of the extra income and then spend the other half on bettering your lifestyle. That way, you live below your means and feel content with your lifestyle too.

16. Use ATMs sparingly. Avoid fees by only using ATMs that are in your bank's network. Consider not using ATMs at all. I create a monthly budget and determine how much cash I would need at the beginning of every new budget period. Then I go to the bank teller and withdraw the exact amount that I need. ATMs can make mistakes, and I would prefer to not waste my time and money cleaning up a mistake that was not my fault. I've always used community banks so their ATMs aren't as fancy as the ones you'd find at bigger banks like Chase Bank or Bank of America where you can deposit cash at the ATM too. I had a roommate who deposited cash via the ATM at TD Bank. The ATM counted the money wrong and deposited it into his account $100 short. He was so angry talking to customer service on the phone and explaining the situation and they wouldn't help him. I sincerely believe him, but how can you successfully argue about a machine malfunctioning to a faceless corporation? Tellers can make errors too—at least you can pin the blame on someone and make the situation right again.

17. Use a community bank or credit union. Community banks and credit unions offer the same services while charging lower fees. I use small banks exclusively because I think big banks require high minimum balances. Every single big bank I researched required at least $1,500.00 to open a checking account. Also, if your account balance ever went below that amount, then you would get charged a monthly fee. On the other hand, every single small bank that I opened a checking account with required only $100.00 to open, required no minimum balance to maintain and charged zero monthly maintenance fees. There is no point in requiring such a high minimum other than letting the bank inflate its assets. I keep only $50.00 as the buffer in my checking account, and I never go below $50.00 or pay an overdraft fee because I follow a budget.

18. Remove overdraft protection from your checking account. Overdraft protection is optional, but banks automatically enroll you in this feature when you open a checking account. Why? Because overdraft fees generate over $30 billion in revenue for banks annually. The biggest argument that banks make for overdraft protection is that it saves you from embarrassment when your transaction gets denied due to insufficient funds. For this perk, banks charge $35.00 for overdraft fees per transaction. Is the shame from a cashier or bookkeeper possibly judging you for not having enough money worth the $35? Quite frankly, if you do not have enough money in your account to pay for something, the transaction should be denied. Treat your checking account balance like it is cash. Once the money runs out, you have no more to spend.

19. Pay cash for most purchases. Cash reduces impulsiveness, and you will never have an overdraft fee paying cash. Spending cash elicits greater psychological pain than paying with debit or credit. That means that every time you spend cash, you feel emotional pain. With debit or credit, money is nothing more than a number that decreases every time you spend. Dun and Bradstreet, an American business services company, found that people spent between 12 to 18 percent more when they used credit cards instead of cash. At McDonald's, the average order total for people paying with credit cards was $7.00 compared to $4.50 for people who paid with cash, according to a study by Dun and Bradstreet (Hurd & Konsko, 2020).

20. Open an American Express Bluebird Card or American Express Serve Free Reloads Card if you cannot open a bank account. Believe it or not, 70 million Americans cannot access traditional financial services, which makes life extremely difficult for them. They do not have access because traditional banks charge monthly maintenance fees unless certain conditions are met. These conditions can be keeping a minimum of $1,000 balance at all times or setting up direct deposit. For example, my husband has an individual checking account with Bank of America and $250 of my paycheck gets direct deposited into his account and then we take $50 to pay our joint credit card to avoid the maintenance fees. We called Bank of America asking if the direct deposit could be $200 as long as the sum was $250+ per month. No—it had to be $250+ per paycheck. Low-income earners living paycheck to paycheck who could really make use of the $1,000 should not have to incur a fee when their balance reaches exactly $0. Employees working for small businesses that still write checks and do not provide direct deposit as an option should not be paying bank fees based on the company they work for. People who do not have regularly scheduled paychecks also lose out. These people must use prepaid cards that cost money to reload. They also pay their utility bills with cash at faraway convenience stores, which wastes gas. The documentary film *Spent: Looking for Change* by American Express exposes the problem in depth. For those who open a bank account, consider opening an American Express Bluebird Card (or Serve Card if you live in NY, TX, or VT, where monthly maintenance fees are waived.) Do not buy the temporary card at a local retailer for $3.95; you can sign up for a personalized card for free online on Bluebird.com or Serve.com. There are three options of Serve cards to choose from. Make sure you choose the green-colored card that specifically has free reloads because the blue-colored card charges $3.95 per cash reload. You can do free cash reloads at any CVS, Dollar General, Family Dollar, Rite Aid, and at participating 7-Eleven and Walmart stores.

21. Have a policy of never lending money to family or friends. Lending money can ruin your relationships. It is possible that your family or friends will never pay you back or pay the money back late. Your relationships become strained because it feels awkward to ask for the money back when you need it, even though it was yours. It is also possible that you and the borrower enter a cycle of chronic lending and borrowing. If the borrower asked you once and you said yes, the borrower might ask for more in the future. Enforce a no-lending policy and treat everyone the same so they do not feel like it is personal when you say no. You can even offer to teach your family and friends how to create a budget and save money so they can learn how to overcome their tough situation without borrowing money from anyone. If you want to give money, give away the money as a gift with no strings attached.

22. Stop dropping your money on the ground. I once had a roommate, Andrei, who complained to me about how he was always broke. A few weeks after moving in, I noticed he constantly dropped quarters all around the house—in the bathroom, in the kitchen, in front of my bedroom door, etc. I picked them up and saved them for myself obviously. No wonder Andrei was always broke. He couldn't even manage his coins. I must have saved $10. What was weird was he had a pile of Russian currency that he left on a windowsill in the common area that I thought was some form of monopoly money. It had been sitting there for weeks and I didn't know who it belonged to, so I cleaned the apartment and tossed the play money in the trash. It turned out to be Andrei's and he blew up on me for throwing out his "precious and irreplaceable" Russian currency given to him by his grandfather, which was unusable here in the United States to buy stuff! Yet he didn't care for dropping perfectly good quarters all over the apartment. In Lubbock, I picked up pennies on the sidewalk about twice a week. Lubbock is a town where everyone drives a car, so I wonder who these people were who constantly dropped their money on the sidewalk.

23. Find free or cheap ways to transfer money. My friend Chung wanted to send $1,500.00 to someone in Orlando, FL. Western Union charged $126.00 in fees for cash pickup at an agent location. When the recipient tried to pick up the cash, Western Union withheld the money because it thought that this transaction was a fraud. Western Union then gave my friend a hard time when he asked for his money back. They asked Chung to prove that he was Chung by asking a bunch of personal questions that they honestly did not need to know the answers to. Honestly, do not use Western Union. There are cheaper ways to transfer money. For one, bank wire transfers are cheaper than Western Union. Another option is to buy a money order for under $3.00 and then mail it via USPS Priority Mail Express 2-Day Flat Rate Envelope for $23.75. Finally, PayPal, Venmo, Cash App, and Zelle are free!

24. Build your credit using a secured credit card. The first question people ask me when I tell them that I live debt free is, "How will you buy a house without any credit history?" I plan on buying a house with cash. If I need a mortgage, then I can go to a bank and use manual underwriting to obtain the loan. Another option is to build a credit history by using a secured credit card. Make a deposit of $500.00. That will be your line of credit and be your collateral for situations where you fail to pay. Every month, charge $10.00 on the secured card and pay the balance on time. If you do not pay on time, the credit issuer takes your deposit. Make sure your issuer reports the card to all three credit bureaus: Equifax, Experian, and TransUnion.

25. File your own tax return. If your financial situation is simple, as in you earn your income through a job and have few deductions, you do not need a tax preparer or CPA. I would not recommend a CPA unless you own multiple businesses or have investments beyond your retirement account. Many people avoid filing their own taxes completely because they are nervous about doing it wrong. Go to the library and borrow a book on how to do your own taxes. Tax return forms from the Internal Revenue Service also come with step-by-step instructions on how to fill out the forms correctly. Doing your taxes manually will teach you exactly how your income tax is determined and see through the lies that politicians spin about taxes. You can also see the various deductions available. I did this for a few years, and it is always a good exercise because knowing the kinds of deductions out there makes me more aware of how my decisions affect my tax liability in the future. The alternative to doing it by hand is to buy tax software, usually for less than $100.00.

26. Be wary of setting up automatic bill pay. Automatic bill pay is convenient, but some companies, not all, are sleazy and take advantage of customers who want to pay their bills on time using this feature. For instance, Lubbock Power & Light and CareCredit change their billing dates every month. A bill might be due on May 12 this month and then on June 10 the next month. If you set up automatic bill pay for the 11th of every month, then you will get charged a late fee. This is unbelievable and unfair! If you really want to set up automatic bill bay, look through all your bills in the last 12 months and look for the earliest due date. Take that due date and minus 3 calendar days. That should be the monthly date you schedule your automatic bill pay to hit.

Chapter 3

Savvy Shopping

27. Stop emotional spending. Some people shop just to get a temporary emotional high after having a bad day at work or a fight with their spouse. Others spend money to fill the emptiness in their lives. Some might spend frivolously because they worked hard for their money and therefore, they think, "I deserve it." Parents might spend thousands of dollars on toys and gadgets for their children because they think it is the best way to show their affection. They think spending lots of money makes up for the fact that they are always at work. Most children just want to spend quality time with their parents and act up to get their attention. Whatever emotional reasoning you use to rationalize your spending habits, acknowledge it and let it go. Find a healthier way to deal with your stress. Nurture your spiritual life without spending money.

28. Be content with what you already have. I think being content is very important when it comes to saving money. Too many people fall into the trap of keeping up with the Joneses. Identify who your Joneses are, figure out why you feel jealousy or envy, and then let those feelings go. Forget about your hot friend on social media who has hundreds of photos and never wears the same outfit twice. Forget about your coworker who went on a two-week vacation to Fiji. Forget about your neighbor who has the biggest house on the block or the newest luxury car. What is the truth behind that glamorous lifestyle? Most likely debt. One man always posted photos on Facebook of himself flying on private jets to exotic countries. How did he afford it? He bought a one-way economy-class flight on a commercial airline to another country. Then he returned on an empty-leg flight on a private jet. Women went gaga over him because they thought he was rich. He was not rich and could never take a woman onboard with him because then his secret would be revealed. Stop trying to impress people. Be grateful for the things you have.

29. Only spend money on things that align with your priorities. Stop spending valuable time and hard-earned money on things you do not like. Only spend money on things are important to you—things you care about. You don't like expensive restaurants? Then don't eat there. Don't like overpriced parking? Then park further away where it's cheaper or find an alternative form of transportation. Don't like high-maintenance women? Then don't date them. Don't like reading? Then don't buy books (but do buy this one because it helps me put food on the table). You waste money when you spend mindlessly.

30. Shop without touching. Touching items in the store increases your emotional attachment to the respective items. Touching merchandise makes you feel like you already own it and makes you value it more. Behavioral economists call this the endowment effect. For instance, Apple openly invites customers to fiddle with iPhones and pencil manufacturers create packages that have holes. Try your best to only look, not touch. Touch with only one finger if you must (University of Chicago Press Journals, 2009).

31. Share an amazon prime membership. Amazon Prime costs $99.00 per year. Split it with a friend and pay only $49.50 per year for free deliveries. Better yet, find a friend who is still a college student so you can get it at an even lower price. Currently, Prime Student costs only $49.00 per year. You are allowed to split your Amazon Prime membership with another adult using their function called Household. The adult could be your roommate, spouse, or even friend living in another city. The only catch is that you must be comfortable agreeing to share payment methods and therefore someone else having access to using your credit card to buy stuff. Share your Prime membership only with someone you trust to use the correct respective credit card when placing orders.

32. Make a quick mental calculation before buying anything. When I first started saving money at 18 years old, I worked as a cashier at ShopRite and got paid minimum wage ($8.00/hour). I hated my job at ShopRite, and I hated the nasty customers who saw me as inferior for working such a low-level job. During this time in my life, everything seemed so expensive to me because I made so little. Before I bought anything, I always calculated how many hours of work it took me to be able to buy an item. For example, a $69.00 backpack would take me nine hours of work to be able to pay for it—nine hours of living hell at ShopRite. I wanted it, so I bought it and I still use it today. But for almost everything else, I told myself no and saved my money instead. That is how I saved $1,000.00 in three months while making minimum wage. Other people would easily drop $100.00 on something, but not me. Work was already hard enough. I couldn't bear to spend my hard-earned money because spending it meant I would stay at the job longer. I would lack the freedom to leave if I depended on my job to support such a lifestyle.

33. Do something correctly the first time around. Sometimes you want to cut corners to save money. I get it. But it is cheaper to do something the right way the first time around. Back when I worked at Economy Hardware, most customers wanted the cheapest prices they could get, which usually meant buying low-quality parts. Low-quality parts broke faster, and those customers almost always had to come back and buy again to replace or repair. They would have saved money by doing things properly from the very beginning. As another example, my friend Susan isn't afraid to pay more money to get a better-quality job done.

One time she scratched her Lexus. She paid a repair shop extra money to make sure that they used original factory paint, not a cheaper brand. The staff said no problem. A few days after the paint job was done, Susan and I were hanging out. It was bright and sunny outside, and we saw that it was not the original factory paint. It was a close match, but the paint had a very slight glitter to it and Susan noticed. No one can cheat Susan, as she can be very meticulous about how something should be done. She demanded that the repair shop redo it for free. The repair shop wasted money in the end because they had to do it twice.

34. Wait 30 days before buying anything that is not a necessity. Make a list of everything you want to buy and write today's date. After 30 days, go back to your wish list. Many times, the urge to shop has passed, and you can cross the items off your list. If you still want something on your wish list, then buy it. No guilt, no shame.

35. Wait until Black Friday or Cyber Monday. Just like waiting 30 days before buying something, keep a wish list and then wait until Black Friday or Cyber Monday. You might get a fantastic deal on a product that you want to buy.

36. Tax yourself. We all have shopping addictions, and that is okay. It becomes not okay when these addictions stop you from progressing financially. Back when I was depressed and had only one friend, I had an addiction to chocolate. Chocolate always made me feel happy, temporarily. But it wasn't good for my health. I exercised a lot to keep my weight in the normal range, but I couldn't fool my doctor. The blood test results showed that there was too much sugar in my blood and my doctor told me to stay away from sweets. Chocolate wasn't good for my wallet either. A bar of chocolate for $3.00 equaled $90.00 per month, since I bought a bar of chocolate every day. I couldn't control myself though, so I started taxing myself on chocolate expenses. Whenever I bought chocolate, I had to make a 100 percent matching contribution to my savings. For instance, if I bought $6.00 worth of chocolate, I had to contribute an extra $6.00 to my savings, in addition to the 25 percent that I saved from every paycheck. With taxation and daily meditation sessions, I quit my chocolate addiction after a few months.

37. Use coupon codes. Sometimes online websites run promotions that you do not know about. Visit RetailMeNot.com and similar sites to see whether the online store you are shopping from has any coupon codes available. You can also get a separate email account to sign up for coupons on sites you shop at often, but sometimes that entails having the login email address being the same as the marketing subscription email address if you are okay with it. I am not okay with that. Lately, I've been using the free Honey browser extension to automatically test various coupon codes in my shopping cart for me, and then use the one with the biggest savings. Since it's free, they probably track all my shopping data on the web and sell it off to data brokers and marketing companies. I do notice I've been getting served more targeted ads ever since, but I feel no compulsion whatsoever to spend money based on an advertisement.

38. Shop with a friend. For BOGO sales where you only need one and not two, shop with a friend. Split the promotion with your friend and then split the bill. You both end up saving money.

39. Shop under a time limit. Give yourself a limited time to shop. That way, you buy only what you need and then leave. The longer you stay at a store, the more tempted you feel to look around and then waste money buying unnecessary merchandise.

40. Know what you already own. A lot of times, people buy duplicates because they are not sure whether they already have the same item at home. I just did this last month with flour. I wanted to bake homemade bread and bought all-purpose flour, but then when I got home, I found out that I already had flour in the pantry. I returned the flour the week after. My ex-boyfriend Jared was a hoarder, and his room was always cluttered. You could never find anything in his room. One time when we cleaned together, we found multiple packs of teeth whitening strips. He kept buying more because he misplaced them. Keeping track of the things you already own will save you time and money.

41. Weigh your options between Amazon and eBay. Both Amazon and eBay are enormous online marketplaces that offer competitive prices. However, check both whenever you want to buy something. Sometimes, eBay might be cheaper than Amazon's already low prices because of sales tax and auctions. Amazon collects sales tax on transactions in all states, but eBay only collects sales tax when the seller is in the same state that the item is being shipped to. eBay also has an auction-style format, so you might win an item at a great price.

42. Use self-checkout. Impulse purchases decrease when customers use self-checkout instead of staffed checkout. The wait time is usually shorter, which means you spend less time looking at the tempting merchandise surrounding the checkout area.

43. Be prepared. Always do your research before going somewhere or buying something. When the information cannot be found online, call the organization, and double-check. When I needed to get my learner permit at the Texas Department of Public Safety, one of the requirements was two documents to prove my residency. I had a copy of my lease. For the second document, I wanted to use my bank statement, but I only had the online statement. I wanted to print it out at FedEx, but my husband told me that I could use the bank statement on my phone or USB flash drive. I believed him, and when I got to the TxDPS, I found out that they only took paper copies. I was livid! I headed home with no learner permit. I wasted $20.05 on car service rides that day.

44. Fall asleep and then stay asleep. When I taught Dave Ramsey's Financial Peace University, I had a student named Lori. Lori had a bad habit of falling asleep and then waking up at 4 AM just to watch infomercials on television. She obsessively bought overpriced junk that she never ended up using. Trust me, that product you see on television is not worth losing your sleep over. Thankfully, Lori canceled her cable sometime after we got acquainted.

45. Negotiate. You can negotiate anything, except death and taxes. Negotiation is a skill you can learn to master, and it can be fun when you are good at it. There are plenty of books on how to negotiate that you can borrow from your local library. One book that I enjoyed reading was *You Can Negotiate Anything* by Herb Cohen. I negotiated with my husband when we chose which condo to submit an offer on. There was a gorgeous 2-bed 1-bath condo in a location that had a short commute for both of us, asking $425,000. My husband totally loved it, but at that price, our new total monthly housing payment would be $2,300. We were paying $1800 in rent, so I demanded a roommate to offset the $500 increase in housing expense. Then we found a condo listed at $260,000 for the same amount of space. It didn't look as nice, but I liked the location for its distance to not just my workplace, but to the Asian grocery store. My husband's commute via public transit would have been much worse though. I knew the second condo was a better deal for our finances long-term. Think of what we could do with that money over the course of 30 years (opportunity cost). So, I negotiated with him and said if we submitted a $295,000 offer ($1,700 monthly payment) on the second condo, I would let him have the second bedroom all for himself, no roommate needed, and eventually save to buy us a second car too. I'd rather spend $12,000 on a 3-year-old used car than pay $130,000 extra on a home. He accepted because we both got what we wanted.

46. Visit your favorite store without any money. Get comfortable with the feeling of temptation and impulsiveness. Without any money to buy anything, you are forced to look at the products without taking them home with you. When you get used to doing this, you will appreciate an item's aesthetic or function without feeling like you need to own it. Doing this also makes you aware of the subtle tricks that stores use to convince customers to buy something, such as advertising, store layout, and product displays. I did this a lot back when I was a teenager, and today I can walk into a store without feeling the need to buy something.

47. Read product reviews. With the internet, anybody can read product reviews before buying. Usually, the reviews can be believed. I like to read both good and bad reviews to get an idea of what I am about to buy. Buy products that are great value for the money spent. Stop wasting your money on products that end up being pieces of junk that cannot be returned after being opened.

48. Buy something and then return it. Sometimes I buy something that I am on the fence about, and then I totally regret my purchase the next day. This is called buyer's remorse. Whenever this happens, I go back to the store with my item and receipt, and I request a refund. I avoid shopping at stores that only give store credit and no refunds. I stopped shopping at Forever 21 a long time ago due to their policies.

49. Make a list before you go shopping for anything. Think of times when you intend on only buying a pair of blue jeans or a pillow at the mall but then come home with three giant bags full of merchandise. You need a shopping list. Stay focused on your goal, which is to buy a specific item and then leave. With a shopping list, your eyes scan the store for specific items on your list and filter everything else out. Shopping lists also ensure you do not miss anything, so you never make a second trip to the store.

50. Know the price. Once, at Walmart, I wanted to buy a bike helmet. I found a comfortable helmet that I liked for $21.00, but then at the cash register, it rang up $35.00. I was caught off guard and said the sign stated $21.00. I thought the cashier was going to physically walk to the helmet section and check the price herself. However, she merely smiled and said, "Okay," and gave it to me for $21.00. Afterward, I doubted whether I saw the right price or not. I do know that I saved $14.00 by refusing to pay $35.00.

51. Keep receipts and mail your rebate forms. Mail-in rebates seem like a great deal, which attracts customers into retail stores. However, most customers never claim their rebates. Over $500 million in rebates go unclaimed annually (Moore, n.d.). People who do claim their rebates tend to forget after eight weeks that they are owed money, so they never call to complain. The manufacturers never mail the rebate money, and then hope that customers forget and won't notice. I would create an event on my Google Calendar 8 weeks from the mail-in date, with email notification turned on. When I get the email in my inbox, I remember to follow up. If that's too tech-savvy for you, you can get a paper tray that holds all your financial-related paperwork (could be parking tickets you are appealing, bills you are negotiating, insurance quotes you are shopping around for—not just a tray for rebates) that's still in processing and use post-it notes with the dates for follow up.

52. Think of the hidden costs of owning something before buying anything. For instance, when you buy books, at first, you only need a small shelf to store them. Over time as you purchase more books, you need a bigger bookshelf. Buy some more, and you will need two bookshelves. Buy even more, and you will need a bigger apartment or house or self-storage unit to store everything! Think of the amount of money it costs to move your stuff too. My friend Bob spent $10,000.00 moving all the possessions that he accumulated over a lifetime from New York City to London. I am just using books as a small example. You might not have a shopping addiction for anything in particular. You might just buy a lot of stuff. Everything you own has a hidden cost of ownership, whether it is for storage, repair, or moving.

53. Think of the nominal value that you save and not the percentage. The nominal value is basically the face value. When you see something for $100.00 and then find out you can buy the same thing for $75.00 at a store one mile away, I bet you will drive one mile to save $25.00. However, when you see something for $10,000.00 and then find out you can buy the same thing for $9,975.00 at a store one mile away, I bet you won't be so quick to go elsewhere for a better deal. That is because most people make a quick mental calculation based on the percentage. While $25.00 out of $100.00 is 25 percent, $25.00 out of $10,000.00 is only 0.25 percent. Driving a mile to save $25 is the same in either situation. You should drive a mile in the second scenario because $25 saved is still $25.

54. Avoid falling for deals and discounts. Deals and discounts entice you to buy things you did not need or want to begin with. You might think you are saving money by buying something when it is on sale. However, if you are buying something just because it is on sale, you aren't saving any money at all. Only buy things that were already on your wish list and then happened to be on sale later. One trick you can do is add items to your online shopping cart and then abandon it. Some retailers will email you a coupon a few days later to entice you to buy. In this scenario, if you still want it a few days later, you're not falling for a deal or discount, because you were probably going to buy it anyway.

55. Avoid falling for manipulative advertisements. Advertisers try to convince consumers that buying a certain product will make them smarter or more attractive. Do not fall for their manipulative tactics. Question the expert opinion, overlook the attractive people, see through the lifestyle that the advertisements try to evoke, and do not fall for the fear that you feel. Visit Unenticed.com to learn how to free yourself from intrusive and manipulative marketing and advertising.

56. Say no to salespeople. Salespeople can be extremely pushy and aggressive. Be polite and use your body language to indicate your disinterest. Firmly say, "Thanks, but no thanks. Have a great day." The last thing you need is a salesperson pressuring you to buy something you do not need and succeeding at it. If you're the kind of person who is susceptible to a good sales pitch, you need to bring a levelheaded friend or partner with you and have them hold your wallet! It's not like you just happen to get bombarded with a sales pitch out of nowhere and thus are not able to plan for it. You're usually a warm lead who is open to hearing about a product or service and opting into a phone call or presentation to hear more about whether it's the right fit for you. Then you get bombarded with all the benefits and features and think, wow this is really amazing. You need someone with you who can think clearly and discuss with you afterward before impulsively handing over your credit card.

57. Use FreeCycle.org. Lots of people registered on FreeCycle give away their things for free because they care about the environment. Join a FreeCycle group in your town or neighborhood. There are also neighborhood groups you can join on Facebook or Nextdoor where members buy, sell, and trade.

58. Abandon your online shopping cart. I like to add products to my Amazon shopping cart and then abandon it. When I visit Amazon again a few days later, maybe even a few weeks later, I often forget that I left products in my shopping cart. If I cannot remember what was in my shopping cart, then chances are I never needed the products in the first place. If I do remember, then I buy it.

59. Use MassDrop.com. My husband is an audiophile who is constantly researching audio equipment so he can buy products with the best value. He wanted to buy the Edifier R1700BT Bluetooth Bookshelf Speakers for $149.00 on Amazon. I thought it was too much money though, so he was willing to settle for the Edifier R1280T Powered Bookshelf Speakers, which cost $99.00 on Amazon. However, after doing some research, he found MassDrop.com. He bought the more expensive speakers for only $99.00! The price was a steal.

60. Join a consumer cooperative. Consumer cooperatives are businesses that belong to the people who use them. They provide services while saving consumers money. Typically, only members of a cooperative can use its services. The members keep the prices low by volunteering. There are many types of consumer cooperatives: credit unions, utility, electric, telephone, housing, food, childcare, insurance, and health.

Chapter 4

Career and Work

Corporate Business

61. Automate your hiring process. Pay for an Applicant Tracking System to filter out job applicants for you instead of fully staffing your Human Resources department. Finding the best person for the job is obviously just as easy as finding the person who matched a checklist of keywords that you got online. When I applied for a personal banker job at Prosperity Bank on 4827 4th Street in Lubbock, I had to apply online. This was an entry-level job in which I met seven out of the eight qualifications. Prosperity Bank rejected my application in 10 hours! I emailed the Lobby Manager, Jacob Tate, and asked him why. Apparently, I did not meet all eight qualifications! A few days later, I walked into a Prosperity Bank branch and asked the employees whether they met all eight qualifications when they got the job. They said they met only half the qualifications. (Dear Prosperity Bank, my rejection is your loss.) Now, if you actually want to hire outstanding employees to help your company grow, you must go through every application by hand. Do not let the software make the decision for you. A computer does not know best when it comes to screening applicants. If you hire using software, I bet you are more likely to get expensive staff turnovers than if you personally screened applications to look for people who will fit the job and your company culture.

62. Slash your workforce by one-third. Lay off your employees and replace them with robots. Overwork your remaining employees by giving them twice the amount of work as before. Make sure they never have time to see their families. It does not matter how poorly you treat your employees so long as you keep raking in revenue to ensure your stock prices go up. For example, JP Morgan Chase Bank laid off 5,000 tellers in 2015 and 2016. They replaced the tellers with ATMs. Employees must be loyal to the company, but the company in no way ever needs to reciprocate such loyalty. This is the mantra of almost all corporations nowadays: profits over people, baby! Now, if you actually want to run an ethical and fair company, keep your workforce as it is and find other ways to cut costs. Southwest Airlines was able to do this during the last recession. I am sure your company can find a way to do likewise. Focus on the long-term consequences, not the short-term savings. Your workforce is the lifeblood of your company. Without a good workforce working at optimum productivity, your company cannot grow. You will lose money in the long term if you only worry about this quarter's numbers.

63. Pay your employees as little as you can get away with. Let your employees survive on minimum wage and government assistance programs. Pay executives their multimillion-dollar bonuses. This is a joke. This may sound counterintuitive: pay your employees above market rate for their responsibilities. This reduces the employee turnover rate. Wages have been stagnant since the 1970s. In order for employees to get the raises they deserve and progress in their careers, they resort to job-hopping. Hiring and training new employees is expensive. That money could go toward paying your employees more for being good at what they do.

64. Move your customer service center to India. Your customers do not mind the fact that your customer service representatives speak little English. Just do not complain when customers rate your company poorly on ConsumerAffairs.com. Poor customer service will affect your revenue in the long run, and not for the better either.

65. Completely automate your phone menu. Everyone loves this infamous line: "Please continue to hold. Your call is very important to us." To save even more money, make it impossible for customers to reach a live customer service representative regardless of which numbers they press on the keypad. Everyone knows that a robot can answer every single question in the entire world. And if a customer hits the 0 key to get an operator, hang up on the phone call automatically and make the customer start all over again. Sooner or later though, everyone will catch on to what your company is doing. Do not be surprised to find that your customers decide to spend their money at a competing company instead.

Small Business

66. Start your own business with as little money as possible. Fail fast and fail cheap. My mom has been a small business owner for the past 22 years. Some of her best business ventures were the ones she started for only $1,000.00. Her worst business was one that she invested a couple of thousand dollars on. The amount of capital you start your business with does not determine how profitable and successful it will be.

67. Hire an independent freelancer instead of using an agency. Freelancers are cheaper than agencies. Many people hire freelance graphic designers for one-time gigs like business card designs and logo designs.

68. File forms yourself. There are so many forms out there that I cannot list them here. However, I can give you examples of how you can save money. For instance, to start a small business under a unique name, you need to get a Certificate of Assumed

Name. You can file this yourself for only $100.00 in New York City, or you could pay someone else to do it for you for $500.00. It is very easy to do it if you are willing to do the research online. My friend Isaac didn't know this and hired someone else to do it. As another example, pretend you are an immigrant, and you want to apply for a green card. The application fees come out to a total of about $2,150.00. The forms are very easy to complete, and all forms have complementary instructions. Also, plenty of websites explain the application instructions in laymen's terms. However, most people get overwhelmed or intimidated, so they pay an immigration lawyer a couple thousand dollars to do it for them, in addition to the application fees.

69. Say no to recruiters persuading you to join a multi-level marketing scheme. Keep your money. Over 99 percent of people in multi-level marketing or network marketing companies report a net loss annually. Why? The business structure is designed to make you fail. While some companies require you to purchase an initial "kit" to start, some other companies tell potential recruits that they do not need to purchase anything, but after joining, they cannot receive their commission payment without reaching a minimum quota. Since most people do not sell enough to reach the quota, they buy their own products to qualify! People in multi-level marketing have basements full of unused products, and they are in credit card debt up to their eyeballs, but they will never tell you that! There is no such thing as getting rich quick like those recruiters want you to believe. People in multi-level marketing who tell you that they make millions of dollars every year and that they want you to achieve the same thing are lying. Visit MLMWatch.org for more information. Do not join. You are better off starting your own small business by finding your own suppliers and customers.

Employees

70. Work part-time instead of full-time. This sounds counterintuitive. For some people, though, working part-time might be able to save them more money than when working full-time. For instance, people who work long hours never have time to cook or take care of their own children. They pay higher prices for convenience foods like restaurant meals or frozen dinner meals. They pay someone else to do their laundry. They pay someone to clean the house. They pay for childcare services. They do not have time to research and find the best deals, so they just pay without thinking. You get the point. People who never have the time end up paying higher prices.

71. Buy your work wardrobe after you get the job. You never know what job you will get next. Buy one quality interview suit and then only buy work clothes after you are completely certain you got the job.

72. Say no to unpaid internships. Unpaid internships make absolutely no sense. In addition to employers profiting from your free slave labor, you also spend money on transportation and clothes out of your own pocket, which can add up. There is no guarantee that you will get a full-time job when the internship ends. Employers make false promises to motivate you. Stop working for free just to get your foot in the door. You devalue your own work when you do this, which makes it harder for you to find employment later. If you want to work for free, then volunteer for a cause that you believe in or work on a cool project in your spare time.

73. Maximize your employer's 401(k) matching contributions. Too many people let this golden opportunity go to waste. For example, let's say your employer matches 50% of your 401(k) contributions, up to the first 6% of your annual gross salary. If your salary is $50,000, then you should make it your goal to contribute $3,000, and then your employer will contribute $1,500, making the total contribution $4,500. You can always contribute beyond the 6% in this example, but if you don't contribute 6%, you are leaving free money on the table. Remember to recalculate how much to contribute when you get a raise. Lastly, if your employer doesn't match, you're better off investing your money with a Roth IRA where your money will grow tax-free. Start thinking about your retirement now.

Chapter 5

Housing

Location

74. Live in the same city as where you work. At Kingsborough Community College, I had a professor who taught Mondays to Thursdays and then lived in Washington, D.C. on Fridays, Saturdays, and Sundays. This was an expensive lifestyle because he paid rent in two different cities and drove at least 450 miles every week traveling back and forth. I do not know why he did that, but he probably should have looked for a teaching job in Washington, D.C. instead.

75. Move to a cheaper place, neighborhood, or city. I was surprised by how much rent differs throughout the United States. In New York City, I paid $750.00 every month for a bedroom the size of a shoebox and shared the apartment with three other people who never cleaned up after themselves. Everyone shared a single bathroom. In Lubbock, my husband and I paid $420.00 every month for our bedroom and private bathroom. Our roommate Amin rented the other bedroom, and aside from playing piano every day, he was mostly quiet. The apartment had a kitchen larger than you would normally find in New York City and had a washer and dryer in the unit. We live in Boston now. Our 2-bed 2-bath Lubbock apartment would cost at least $2,400.00 in Boston.

76. Find inexpensive ways to move across the country. Before moving, sell, donate, and trash the things you no longer need or use. This reduces cardboard boxes, fuel, and shipping fees. With everything that is left, pack them into boxes and move them yourself by car or ship them. You can ship via USPS, UPS, and FedEx. Choose the company that gives you the lowest quote. You can also try shipping with Amtrak or Greyhound, which is cheaper than standard shipping service. The only drawback to Amtrak and Greyhound is that you must drop off and pick up at the train/bus station, instead of having it delivered straight to your new home.

77. Buy a house in an Italian village for 1 euro. Over the years, various Italian villages have been offering to sell homes for 1 euro, under the condition that you invest your money to renovate. These villages have a small, elderly population, so they are looking for adults under 40 years old to rejuvenate the town and create jobs.

78. Move to a developing country. The cost of living is lower, and your money can stretch further. The biggest factor to overcome is fear of change and fear of getting robbed and stabbed. But hey, we have mass shootings all the time here in the United States, so it's not like it's any better here in The States either.

Mortgage

79. Buy a smaller house. A smaller house requires less upkeep. For one, you use less gas and electricity. You buy less stuff in general, as there is no space to put anything. You also spend less time cleaning the place. Big houses require hiring a professional cleaner at least every other week.

80. Buy a less expensive house. Save money on homeowners insurance and property taxes.

81. Buy a house through Habitat for Humanity. The average cost of a Habitat home is only $90,000.00. Habitat homeowners make a $500.00 down payment and make monthly payments no more than 30 percent of their income. Moreover, they pay almost no interest on the mortgage. To buy a Habitat home, you must complete 400 hours of sweat equity toward the building of Habitat homes. There is no waiting list. You have to complete your sweat equity hours first, which could take over a year, and then you get matched with a home. How long it takes to get approved is driven by the availability of developed properties. Pace of construction is dependent on fundraising and other factors. Contact your local Habitat for Humanity for more information.

82. Buy a house that is below market value. Consider off-market property. Also, find out when your local courthouse holds auctions so you can bid on foreclosed homes.

83. Put down 20 percent or more for the mortgage. Liz and Nick, a newly married couple from Pennsylvania, attended my personal finance seminar. Their relatives boasted about how they obtained their mortgages with no down payment, so Liz and Nick wanted to do the same. It sounded like a great idea, but it was not. It was stupid. By putting zero down, you take out a mortgage that is tens of thousands of dollars more, which is nothing to laugh about. You end up paying more in interest. Also, when you do not put down at least 20 percent, you must pay for private mortgage insurance.

84. Borrow a 15-year mortgage instead of a 30-year mortgage. You would pay significantly less in interest on the 15-year mortgage than on the 30-year mortgage. Some people argue that mortgage interest is tax-deductible. Use the 15-Year vs. 30-Year Mortgage Calculator on www.NerdWallet.com to compare the monthly payment amounts and see how much in interest you would save over the life of the loan. You will most likely save more by paying off your mortgage early, instead of prolonging your mortgage and deducting the interest from your taxes.

85. Refinance your mortgage. Refinance to get a lower interest rate, but first, make sure the cost to refinance is worth it.

86. Make one extra mortgage payment per year. An extra annual payment on your mortgage makes a huge difference over a period of several years. Take your annual bonus and income tax refund and put it toward the principal balance of your mortgage. This could save you more than $10,000.00 in interest payments and could knock years off your loan.

87. Make biweekly payments toward your mortgage. When you pay monthly, you pay only 12 times per year. However, when you pay every other week, you end up paying 26 times per year, because there are 52 weeks in a year. By doing this, you make a full extra payment every year without even realizing it.

88. Choose fixed interest rate over variable interest rate. A variable interest rate starts out low to entice customers, but the interest rate will increase in the future. No one knows when or by how much, but even a small increase has a huge impact. A small percentage of a six-figure loan is a lot of money. With a fixed interest rate, you know you get the same interest rate for the entire term of your mortgage.

89. Compare renting to owning. Renting is not always a money pit. Whether owning is better than renting depends on where you live in the United States and how long you plan on staying in one location. Read the article, "Renting is Throwing Money Away… Right?" by Paula Pant on AffordAnything.com. Paula clearly explains the reasoning and logic behind why renting might be a better option.

Real Estate Taxes

90. Check your property card for mistakes. Check for clerical and misclassification errors that could increase your property taxes. The real estate assessor might incorrectly report the number of bedrooms and bathrooms, the room sizes, or the total square footage.

91. Appeal your property assessment. If your home is valued at 5 percent more than comparable homes in your neighborhood, there is a strong case that your home is overvalued. Make sure you file your appeal before the deadline. Surprisingly, less than 5 percent of homeowners appeal their property assessment, even though assessments are subjective.

92. Find out whether your home improvement or remodeling project qualifies for a tax credit or deduction. See an accountant or use an online calculator to determine how much money you save before starting the project.

93. Avoid building structural improvements to your home. Structural improvements increase your property taxes.

Home Repairs and Maintenance

94. Set aside money every month for home repairs. As a homeowner, you should plan and save for home repairs instead of taking out a home equity loan to pay for emergencies. Major appliances and household systems have a lifespan. Roofs and air conditioning systems need to be replaced every 20 years. Furnaces and dishwashers need to be replaced every 10 years. Water heaters need to be replaced every 5 to 10 years. As an example, the national average cost for a new roof in the United States is $8,154. To save for the new roof, set aside $33.98 per month or $407.70 per year for 20 years. This is a relatively small expense when you think of it like this.

95. Negotiate with contractors. Avoid hiring contractors that offer very low prices, as you might need to hire another contractor to fix the mistakes. Get quotes from three to four reputable contractors. Ask the contractors to separate the cost of the materials from the cost of the labor. Ask whether you can purchase the materials on your own, as you might find a better price. Make sure you do not go too low. Contractors work hard to make their living, and they deserve to get paid too.

96. Do some home repairs and upgrades yourself. My friend Susan is my role model. In 2016, her refrigerator needed a repair after her boyfriend spilled wine inside her refrigerator. The refrigerator smelled like burnt rubber. Susan hired someone to repair it, but it still was not fixed. She got impatient and fixed it herself. I was amazed because not many people take matters into their own hands or have the willingness to learn.

The following repairs and upgrades are easy to learn:

- Changing HVAC filters
- Fixing leaky faucets
- Caulking the tub and shower
- Inspecting the sump pump
- Updating light bulbs
- Installing a programmable thermostat
- Inspecting electrical outlets and cords
- Replacing smoke detector batteries
- Fixing running toilets
- Wrapping the water heater
- Sealing leaky doors and windows
- Flushing the hot water heater
- Beefing up attic insulation
- Installing weather stripping
- Stringing a clothesline
- Repairing a dishwasher
- Fixing a freezer

- Repairing a washer and dryer
- Replacing a faucet
- Updating a bathroom
- Installing a new floor
- Fixing a computer
- Repairing a laser printer

97. Paint your own house. Painting is a skill that you can learn how to do yourself. Watch videos on YouTube on how to paint a wall the right way. The only drawback is that it is time-consuming. You also need to buy the paint and the supplies at your local hardware store.

98. Renovate your own home. Be your own contractor.

99. Do not install a pool or buy a house with a pool. Pools require electricity, water, chemicals, toys, and replacement parts. A pool easily costs hundreds or thousands of dollars every year in maintenance costs. Think like my friend Robert. One day while on a phone call with him, I asked him what he was doing. Robert said, "I'm hanging out by my pool." I did not know Robert had a pool, so I asked him to explain. Robert laughed and said, "My pool is the ocean! It is absolutely free!"

100. Prevent a house fire. A fire can destroy your property. I once met a homeless person in Chicago and asked him why he was homeless. His house caught on fire, and he had no money to rebuild it. His wife and kids were living with his in-laws, but since his in-laws disliked him, he was not welcome. Prevent a house fire by installing smoke detectors and sprinklers. Keep a fire extinguisher nearby. Make sure no one smokes in your house.

101. Shop around for home improvement products. Compare prices at Walmart, Costco, Lowes, Home Depot, and Sam's

Club, along with local hardware stores where you can ask for a discount.

102. Shop at Habitat for Humanity ReStores for home improvement and repair materials. Habitat for Humanity ReStores are nonprofit stores that sell materials to the public at a fraction of the retail price.

103. Search for manufacturer rebates on equipment and supplies. When you do home repairs and upgrades yourself, you sometimes need to use special equipment. Look on the manufacturer's website or at store flyers for rebates. You can also rent tools from hardware stores instead of buying them.

104. Use salvaged materials. Spend a couple of days searching through home rebuilding centers and salvage yards. Be creative and repurpose the things you find. Find new uses for home furnishings and raw materials.

105. Build your roof with roofing samples. It might look ridiculous, and you might become the laughingstock in your neighborhood, but who cares?

106. Paint your walls with paint samples. Angel and Orlando Durr on *Extreme Cheapskates* painted their bedroom using free paint samples. They were not exactly free—Angel negotiated the paint samples down from $3.99. They got paint samples from almost every hardware store in town.

107. Use free or low-cost mulch. Some counties offer free or low-cost mulch.

Homeowners' Association Dues

108. Find out how much are the monthly dues for the Homeowners' Association before buying a house. The monthly dues can be expensive, especially in gated communities.

When my mom was considering buying a house in Seagate, a gated community by the beach in Brooklyn, NY, the monthly dues were way too high. First, all the houses were overpriced and had basements that were damaged by flooding during Hurricane Sandy in 2012. Second, she would have to pay for front gate security, sanitation, maintenance, access to the private beach, and keys. The Homeowners' Association changed the key cards for the front gate every year, and my mom would have to pay $500.00 for four new key cards annually. The key cards could not be duplicated either, so forget about trying to skimp and save on key copies.

109. Analyze the financial reports of your Homeowners' Association. Review the budget and expense reports to see where your money goes. Maybe you can negotiate your Homeowners' Association dues when you find unnecessary expenses.

Rent

110. Be an assistant property manager. In college, I worked as an assistant property manager for a few months in exchange for free rent. The free rent was good because I was unemployed at the time and living off my savings while attending community college. Unfortunately, when the business closed, I had to move back in with my parents until I finished my college degree.

111. Live with your parents. It is not uncommon for people to live with their parents until they are 30 years old nowadays. With student loan debt, Millennial and Gen Z college graduates are forced to live with their parents to make the most of their income. There is no shame in that. Hey, I even know a home improvement contractor named Jean who still lives with his mom, and he is 50 years old! He saves a ton of money. At that age, people call him a mama's boy, though.

112. Live in a basement. I once met a truck driver who lived in a basement in Park Slope, a very expensive neighborhood in

Brooklyn, NY. His rent was dirt cheap, and he saved a ton of money while earning a six-figure income working for an oil company. He was well into his 40s, never planned on getting married, and was away on the road half the time, so where he lived did not really matter. If living in a basement fits into your lifestyle, then go for it.

113. Become live-in help. In exchange for free rent, offer to help around the house and cook meals. Elderly people who live alone usually like this kind of agreement.

114. Live with a roommate. Divide the rent and utilities in half. Make sure you pick roommates who clean up after themselves.

115. Negotiate the rent. Knowledge is power. Research the rent prices of similar places in the neighborhood and go from there.

116. Refer your friends to your apartment. Some property management companies pay tenants who refer their friends. It depends on where you live. I never saw this in New York City, since housing was always in high demand. However, I saw these kinds of promotions in Lubbock, especially for apartment complexes near the Texas Tech University campus.

117. Move to a cheaper apartment when your lease ends. Even if you can only find another apartment with asking rent that is $100.00 lower than your current rent, you still save $1,200.00 every year.

118. Terminate your current lease if it is worth it. Sometimes you save more money by paying the early termination fee and moving to a new apartment with cheaper rent.

119. Get a long-term lease. Commit to a lease for several years. Tenant turnover is expensive for landlords, because every time a tenant leaves, the landlord must paint and repair the rental for the new tenant. In between tenants, the rental remains vacant and brings in no money. Landlords save money with long-term leases, and they pass the savings to tenants in the form of lower rent.

120. Know the law. Do not let landlords take advantage of you by requiring a six-month security deposit or by charging extra fees on top of the standard first month's rent, last month's rent, and security deposit. Know your rights as a tenant and know what is illegal in your state.

Housing Alternatives

121. House sit. Some people travel around the world by house-sitting and never paying another dime in rent again. Homeowners need people to look after their home or pet while they are away. In exchange, you can stay in their home for free.

122. Sleep at a homeless shelter. My friend Charles in Washington, D.C., has been homeless for decades and likes it. He has a permanent bed at a men's homeless shelter and never works. Strangers pay him enough to support his low-cost lifestyle.

123. Squat in an abandoned building. Make sure you do not get caught.

124. Commit a crime. At least criminals get free shelter in prison.

125. Live in a tent. Good luck when it rains.

126. Live in a pineapple under the sea. SpongeBob SquarePants must have the cheapest house in the world.

127. Sleep under a cardboard box. Do this when you have no alternative.

Chapter 6

Utilities

Electricity and Gas

128. Keep your monthly electric bills. It is hard to tell whether you are saving any money if you do not have your electric bills on hand. Try out all these tips and see how much money you are saving.

129. Compare prices from different electrical companies. You can only do this if you live in a city or town that allows competition. If you do not, then you are out of luck. I met an Uber driver who never turned on the lights, used the dishwasher, or turned on the thermostat when he first moved into his Lubbock apartment. The only electricity he consumed was for the six loads of laundry he washed during the first month and the short showers he took. His electric bill from Lubbock Power & Light was $350.00! He was out of luck, as LP&L holds a monopoly in Lubbock. And when I lived in Lubbock, I was out of luck too.

130. Install solar panels. A solar power system costs from $11,000.00 to $15,000.00 to install in your home. However, after that, you only need to pay for electricity when the solar panels do not generate enough power to cover 100 percent of your electricity use. Having a solar system means you no longer remain a victim of electricity rates that increase by 2.2 percent annually. Over a 20-year period, the savings would pay for itself. In some states where electricity rates are extremely high, the savings would be even greater.

131. Use energy-efficient devices. Check for an Energy Star or an energy class label.

132. Turn off all electronic devices when not in use. This includes your television and your computer. You waste hundreds of dollars per year by leaving them on. I am guilty of leaving my laptop on at night because I am too lazy to start it up and wait five minutes in the morning. I have gotten better at turning it off more often though. By the way, with quarantining and working from home, please don't leave your TV on 24/7.

133. Unplug devices when you are not using them. Electronics still draw energy when they are turned off but still plugged in. This is called phantom energy. According to Energy Star, a program run by the U.S. Environmental Protection Agency and the U.S. Department of Energy, "Seventy-five percent of the electricity used to power home electronics is consumed while the products are turned off" (EnergySage, 2021). Unplugging devices might be inconvenient, so buy a power strip and flip the switch instead.

134. Turn off the lights when you leave the room. This is very easy to do.

135. Use energy-efficient light bulbs. LED and CFL light bulbs use less electricity than incandescent light bulbs. They also last much longer. They cost more than regular light bulbs, but you save more money long-term.

136. Use lower-wattage bulbs when you cannot switch to energy-efficient light bulbs. Every room in your house serves a different function, which means some rooms need brighter lighting while others do not.

137. Install and use dimmer switches. Dimmer switches let you control the brightness level. Sometimes you do not need to turn on your lights at the fullest brightness. Dimmer switches also extend the life of the bulb.

138. Paint your rooms with a bright color. Brighter walls reflect more light, which means you need less electrical light to make your room bright.

139. Rent a top-floor apartment with lots of windows. This lets more sunlight into the house. My husband and I once rented an apartment on the first floor. Not enough sunlight came in through the windows because the parking lot adjacent to our unit had a roof. The roof blocked almost all sunlight from coming in. We turned on the lights even during the day.

140. Go to bed earlier at night. Going to bed earlier means you leave your lights on for a shorter duration.

141. Keep your refrigerator and freezer full of food. A full refrigerator and freezer operate more efficiently. Whenever you open the door, cold air escapes and warm air enters. Keeping the refrigerator and freezer full means that less air gets exchanged due to less space.

142. Defrost refrigerators and freezers. When ice builds up, your refrigerator and freezer work harder and use more energy.

143. Set your refrigerator and freezer to the right temperature. You can set your refrigerator to 39 degrees Fahrenheit and your freezer to 5 degrees Fahrenheit. This is the warmest temperature in which bacteria growth is inhibited while electricity usage is minimized. Check the temperature using a thermometer.

144. Defrost food in the refrigerator. Do not defrost food in the microwave. It does not cost you extra to defrost food in the refrigerator. It just takes longer.

145. Only preheat the oven when you need to. Some food recipes, such as casseroles, are very forgiving when you do not preheat. You just need to bake the food for a little longer. Desserts must be baked in a preheated oven. There is no way around it.

146. Keep the oven door closed while cooking. I am guilty of opening the oven door way too often while I am baking. I get too excited, so I constantly check on the food. The truth is I only need to check the food when it is close to being finished. Too bad every time I open the oven door, a ton of the heat gets lost.

147. Use the oven several times if it is already hot. For example, if you use the oven for baking a casserole, then use it for baking cookies afterward. You only preheat once instead of twice.

148. Turn off the oven ten minutes before the food is ready. The oven continues to stay hot even after you turn it off and don't open the door. Again, this only works for forgiving food recipes—not baked desserts.

149. Leave the oven door open after using it and then turn it off during the winter. Since you were using the oven anyway, you might as well use the oven to heat your house. This is not safe when the oven is still on! You can't save money if you're dead from CO2 poisoning.

150. Bake with glass and ceramic cookware. With glass and ceramic cookware, you can reduce your oven temperature by 25 degrees Fahrenheit. The food cooks just as fast.

151. Use a convection toaster oven. Convection toaster ovens are more energy-efficient and time efficient than regular ovens.

152. Cover pots and pans with lids while cooking. This traps the heat, and therefore reduces heat loss.

153. Chop your vegetables into smaller pieces. Finely chopped vegetables cook quicker, reducing the amount of energy needed to cook them.

154. Use only as much water as you need when cooking. More water requires more energy to heat and increases the cooking time.

155. Mow your lawn with a push reel mower. You might even cut your grass in a shorter amount of time, as it is easier to maneuver. A push reel mower requires no gas or starting mechanism. Just walk and push.

156. Mow your lawn less often. Cut your grass based on the length instead of following a set frequency. It is healthier this way. Depending on the weather, sometimes grass grows faster, and sometimes grass grows slower.

157. Do the laundry during off-peak hours. Electricity is cheaper during off-peak hours. Visit your electricity provider's website to find out when the off-peak hours are.

158. Lower the temperature on your water heater. The EPA recommends setting your water heater to 120 degrees Fahrenheit. Your water heater should only be set to 140 degrees Fahrenheit for certain circumstances.

159. Install door sweeps. Door sweeps insulate your home by preventing air from leaking under the door. Door sweeps cost only $10.00, and they are easy to install.

160. Use insulated curtains over your windows. Insulated curtains keep warm air in during the winter and keep hot air out during the summer.

161. Install a programmable thermostat. A programmable thermostat allows you to set a heating and cooling schedule based on when you wake up, when you are home, when you are out, and when you sleep. You never need to remember to adjust the thermostat throughout the day.

162. Lower the thermostat down at night in the winter. Keep warm by layering blankets when you sleep and covering your head with a nightcap. This is how people kept warm before central heating became available. If this is not enough, consider using a heated mattress pad.

163. Use a space heater in the winter. Lower your thermostat. It is unnecessary to heat the entire house when you mainly stay in one room.

164. Set your furnace thermostat to 68 degrees Fahrenheit in the winter. This temperature still feels comfortably warm.

165. Lower your furnace thermostat by a few degrees while you are at work in the winter. No one is home anyway, so there is no reason to keep the thermostat so high.

166. Move furniture away from windows. Sitting near the windows feels cold.

167. Paint your roof white. Homes with white roofs reduce their air conditioning bill by up to 20 percent.

168. Plant a tree for shade. Trees block sunlight from heating the walls and the roof of your home. By keeping your house cool, you reduce the need for air conditioning and you only have to wait 100 years for the tree to be large enough!

169. Open and shut your windows at the right time during the summer. During the summer, open your windows in the evening. Then early in the morning, before the sun heats the day, close your windows and draw the shades to keep the heat out. This keeps your house cool much longer.

170. Use fans instead of air conditioning. Americans are addicted to air conditioning. Am I the only American who can live without it, except when it is over 100 degrees Fahrenheit outside? On a normal summer day, the air conditioner uses the most electricity compared to all appliances. An air conditioner running for 12 hours a day costs around $40.00 per month to operate. A fan running for the same amount of time costs only around $3.50 per month to operate. The difference is huge.

171. Wear a cooling scarf. Soak the cooling scarf in ice water for five minutes, wring out the water, and it is ready to wear. The cooling scarf can keep you cool for hours and decrease your dependency on air conditioning.

172. Set your air conditioner thermostat to 78 degrees Fahrenheit in the summer. Each degree below 78 degrees Fahrenheit uses between 3 to 5 percent more energy.

173. Remove humidity from the air. Your air conditioning thermostat does not need to be set so low if you control the indoor humidity better. When humidity is too high, sweat does not evaporate as quickly, making people feel hot and sweaty. When humidity is low, people feel cooler, even when the temperature is the same. Generally, if your air conditioner is on and your hands feel clammy, then that means the humidity level is too high. Try using DampRid Moisture Absorber to reduce humidity in your home. Do not use an electric dehumidifier, as it uses too much electricity.

Water

174. Shower with your significant other. Save water, shower together!

175. Take showers instead of baths. A five-minute shower uses up to 10 gallons of water, while a bath uses up to 25 gallons of water.

176. Take shorter showers. Reduce your shower time by four minutes, and you can save 4,000 gallons of water every year.

177. Take military showers. Shower out of a bucket. It is fast and uses the least amount of water.

178. Install a low-flow showerhead and low-flow toilet. This can reduce the flow of water by up to 50 percent.

179. Install a faucet aerator. This reduces the water flow without reducing the water pressure.

180. Use cold water for everything except showers. Use cold water for washing laundry, hands, and dishes.

181. Turn off your faucet when shaving or when brushing your teeth. Fill a cup with water instead of letting the water run the entire time.

182. Let your faucets drip when the outside temperature is below 32 degrees Fahrenheit. You pay extra for water, but you avoid paying for a burst water pipe.

183. Repair leaky faucets. Leaky faucets cost money to repair, but you waste water by letting a leaky faucet continually leak. Whenever we had a leaky faucet, my dad denied there was anything wrong. He would let the faucet leak and leak until it got so bad that it needed to be fixed. Quite frankly, I could not understand why, as we rented and it's not like we were the ones paying for a plumber.

184. Use a sink stopper when washing dishes by hand. That way, the water does not run constantly.

185. Avoid using the rinse/hold feature on your dishwasher. This setting uses up to seven gallons of hot water.

186. Skip rinsing the dishes before putting them in the dishwasher. You technically do not need to rinse. Scraping large chunks of food into the trash will suffice. If you still want to rinse, use cold water.

187. Use dishwashers when they are fully loaded. A full load uses the same amount of water as a partial load.

188. Flush your toilet only when needed. If it is yellow, let it mellow. If it is brown, flush it down.

189. Pee in the shower. You use water while showering anyway. You might as well save yourself an extra toilet flush.

190. Use someone else's toilet. My mom has a friend who owns a house with no mortgage and spends an enormous amount of money on private test prep for her children. However, she is a cheapskate who does not want to pay for water. She uses the toilet immediately after arriving at a café or at a friend's house. She does this every single morning. At first, my mom did not notice, but she eventually caught on.

191. Wash your car less often. One car wash uses up to 100 gallons of water.

192. Sweep sidewalks instead of spraying with water. You save 80 gallons of water per year by sweeping instead of spraying.

193. Collect rainwater. Use the rainwater to water your plants and wash your car.

194. Water your lawn less often. In the summer, you only need to water your lawn every 5 to 7 days and in the winter, every 10 to 14 days. When it rains heavily, you can go another two weeks without watering your lawn.

195. Water your lawn, plants, and garden in the early morning, late afternoon, or evening. Avoid watering when it is windy or very sunny, as a large amount of water gets lost through evaporation.

196. Avoid using the garbage disposal. The disposal requires water for it to work. Put your food scraps into a compost bin or trash bag instead.

Trash

197. Create less garbage. Some trash collection companies charge per bag or charge a flat rate for a certain number of bags. When you go over the limit, the company charges additional fees. Lower the amount of garbage bags by not creating garbage in the first place. Shop less and recycle, reuse, or repurpose what you can.

198. Use bigger trash bags. Buy 30-gallon black bags. You can fit more trash, and the trash collection companies still count them as one bag.

199. Buy in bulk. This cuts down on the packaging.

200. Buy fresh foods. This reduces the number of cardboard boxes that go in the trash.

201. Compost food and yard waste. Compostable materials make up 30 percent of the trash that we throw away. Grass clippings, vegetable waste, fruit scraps, coffee grounds, tea bags, eggshells, spoiled milk, cereals, dead leaves, branches, and twigs are compostable.

202. Take your garbage to the dump. You can eliminate your monthly garbage bill completely by taking it to the dump, instead of paying for the service.

203. Shop around if you use private trash collection. When you have several companies to choose from, you can negotiate prices. Ask each company about all the plans they have available. If you follow the tips above, you might get away with using the least expensive plan.

204. Split the garbage bill. Ask your neighbors whether they want to share the garbage bill. This works well if you pick a plan with a flat rate for a certain number of bags. Split the number of bags evenly among the number of households. Choose one house as the pickup point. Everyone drops off his or her trash there for pickup.

205. Commit an entire community to using one trash collection company. You can get lower group rates, and the trash collection company makes more profit due to higher volume.

206. Burn your trash. In some areas, this is legal. You do save money, but I would not recommend it, as the smoke can negatively affect your health.

Phone

207. Scrutinize your phone bill every month. Sometimes third-party companies make unauthorized charges on your phone bill for services you do not use. This is called cramming. Thoroughly review your phone bill from start to finish, especially the fine print. When you see charges that you do not understand, call your provider and ask about it. It just might be that those charges do not belong there, and you can get your money back.

208. Block all third-party charges. If you never purchase ringtones, games, or apps on your phone, then block all third-party charges. That way, you never deal with customer service for unauthorized or fraudulent charges.

209. Bundle services. When you bundle your home phone, cell phone, cable, or internet with one provider, you can get a discount.

210. Negotiate. Call your service provider to ask for a better deal. You will most likely get it, as your service provider does not want to lose you as a customer.

211. Drop unnecessary features from your landline service. Call waiting and caller ID are not necessary. Drop the call waiting, so you can give your full attention to the person you are already talking to. As for caller ID, if you get a telemarketer, then just hang up. As an example of how much you would save, AT&T offers Complete Choice Basic for $40.00 per month, which includes unlimited local calling, caller ID, and call waiting. AT&T also has Standard Home Phone Service for $33.00 per month, which only includes unlimited local calling. You can save $84.00 per year by opting for the standard plan.

212. Drop your landline altogether. I do not see any reason to have a landline unless you do not use a cell phone.

213. Use magicJack or Ooma Telo. These two companies are a great replacement for landlines. You pay an upfront cost for the device and then pay less than $5.00 per month for unlimited domestic phone calls in the United States.

214. Make calls using Skype and WhatsApp. With Skype, you can drop your landline and your cell phone altogether. Buy a Skype Number for $39.00 per year and then buy the United States Unlimited Minutes subscription for $35.88 per year. The total for an entire year is $74.88, which is already what some people pay in cell phone bills for one month.

215. Live without a cell phone. I understand not everyone can live without a cell phone, especially people working in business or sales. Surprisingly, 9 percent of Americans still live without a cell phone. Cell phones have drawbacks. They encourage people to make plans and then cancel at the last minute. Back when cell phones did not exist, people planned ahead of time and were expected to be at a certain place at a certain time. Otherwise, they would not see each other. Cell phones have also made people lonelier—absence presence, being physically present but not mentally present, is a modern problem. By living without a cell phone, your social interactions improve, and you save money in the process.

216. Take care of your cell phone. Too many people drop their cell phones. Back in 2009, my friend Celine dropped her iPhone into the toilet. How does that even happen? I also had plenty of friends who dropped their iPhones on concrete and had spider web cracks on the glass screen. I still do not understand why, in this day and age, people carry their smartphones without a protective case. When you use an Otterbox or Lifeproof protective case, you can drop your phone from multistory buildings and your phone will still come out intact. At the very minimum, you should cover it with a screen protector. Repairing cell phones or buying new cell phones is expensive. Please take extra good care of your cell phone.

217. Use a flip phone. You can only call or text but isn't that the main purpose of cell phones anyway? Their battery life is also longer, so you pay less for electricity. My old flip phone could last for five days before needing another charge.

218. Pay for your cell phone outright. Some cell phone companies lure you into two-year contracts by promising a free cell phone. Actually, the cell phone is not free—you are financing the cell phone. The company charges you more per month compared to people who paid for their phones outright. For instance, for a new $650.00 cell phone, you would pay $27.08 per month for the next two years on top of your regular cell phone plan. Some companies even lock you into a contract and do not allow you to switch carriers until the phone is fully paid off. They also make it difficult for you to pay it off by not allowing you to raise your monthly payments. Instead, they require you to make one payment that pays it off entirely.

219. Buy an older iPhone on eBay. Back in 2015, my phone broke. Money was tight because I was unemployed, so I bought a refurbished iPhone 4S on eBay for $94.95. The phone lasted me for an entire year before the battery's lifespan shortened dramatically to the point it was no longer usable. Today, you can buy a refurbished Apple iPhone 8 64GB for $169.99. The price is affordable compared to a brand-new iPhone.

220. Buy smartphones with less storage. Smartphones with less storage cost less. Sure, you might not be able to download a ton of apps, but do you need that many apps anyway? Apple iPhone SE 2020 is available in three capacity options: the 64 GB for $399.00, the 128 GB for $449.00, and the 256 GB for $549.00. They do this to make the base model price look affordable. The extra $50.00$150.00 for larger storage capacity is mostly profit for Apple. I used an Apple iPhone SE (1st Generation) 16GB for $399.00 (back when this option was still available), and the storage space was enough for my needs. Now I have the Apple iPhone SE (2nd Generation) 128 GB. It's not the base model, but now that I have a YouTube channel, I do need that extra storage to record long videos when I don't have my camcorder with me.

221. Use a smartphone with no service plan connected. You can still use a smartphone if there is a SIM inserted but no service plan connected. Dialing 911 for emergencies will still work. When you have WiFi access, you can contact friends and family using free apps. For instance, I know homeless people who do this. They have no service plans attached to their cell phones, but I can still contact them through Facebook Messenger or WhatsApp. If you're wondering how I know so many homeless people, it's because even back when I made minimum wage, I would buy meals for homeless people in New York City and in other cities I traveled to. We would eat together, and I would listen to their stories on how they got to where they were. I felt poor back then living on minimum wage, but this was a reminder there were people out there even more down on their luck than me and to be grateful for everything I had. People living paycheck to paycheck are just one paycheck away from being homeless.

222. Go prepaid. Prepaid cell phone plans are cheaper than contract plans. Also, with prepaid, you can flexibly switch to another carrier, whereas with a contract you must pay early termination fees.

223. Buy your prepaid phone plans from Calling-Mart.com. When you sign up for an account on CallingMart, you are automatically enrolled in their rewards program. Whenever you purchase prepaid plans from CallingMart, you accrue reward points, which can be used toward any of your future purchases. I saved a couple of dollars per year with the rewards program.

224. Buy your SIM cards online. When I wanted to open a Lycamobile prepaid phone plan for my sister, we went to a local cell phone store first. The owner wanted to charge us $25.00 for the SIM card and to pay a minimum of $100.00 for minutes and texting. I said no. I went on Amazon and bought the same SIM card for $0.01. Then I went on CallingMart.com and paid $10.00 for my sister's prepaid phone plan. She does not call or text often, so $100.00 was too much for her needs.

225. Minimize your data usage. If you have limited data, turn off your data connection when you have free WiFi available. Then turn it back on when you have no WiFi connection. Avoid paying for more data than you need.

226. Go without data. I used to think I could never go without data. In 2017, I did not pay for data. I used my computer for almost everything, and I mainly used my cell phone when I had access to WiFi. Although this sounds inconvenient, I liked it because I focused much more on the people around me. My cell phone plan was only $12.94 per month back then.

227. Consider how you call toll-free numbers. Avoid calling toll-free numbers from cell phones if you have limited minutes every month. Call using a friend's cell phone that has an unlimited calling plan or just use a landline. That way, if you are put on hold for too long, you are not wasting your minutes.

228. Dial 1800FREE411 for free directory assistance service. Telephone companies charge $1.00 or more each time you call directory assistance. In the United States, customers place about six billion 411 phone calls per year. This is a multibillion-dollar industry! You must listen to a short advertisement when you call 1800FREE411, but hey, you can save your money.

229. Track your minutes. If you are a Chatty Cathy and you use a limited calling plan like I do, then track your minutes. Regularly login to your carrier's website and check how many minutes you have remaining.

230. Get rollover minutes. If you have a minute-based plan, opt for a plan that rollovers unused minutes month to month.

231. Pay only for the mobile services you need. I used to use Lycamobile's $19.00 monthly phone plan before its customer service went downhill. Today I use Tello Mobile. The great thing about Tello Mobile is that their phone plans are fully customizable, so you only pay for the mobile services you need. In 2017, I paid $12.94 every month for 500 minutes, which was more than enough for me. I decided to go without texting, as there are plenty of smartphone apps that allow me to text for free instead. I use Facebook Messenger, LINE, WhatsApp, and WeChat. In 2020, I paid $15.69 for a Tello Mobile phone plan with unlimited minutes, unlimited texting, and 2 GB data.

232. Ask for a senior discount. Individuals over the age of 55 might be eligible for a senior discount for their phone plans. Oftentimes, it is not advertised so call customer service and ask.

233. Skip the cell phone insurance. You pay $7.00 per month for two years with no guarantee that you will use the service. When you do claim your loss, you also need to pay $200.00 in deductibles. There is no guarantee you will get a newer or better phone either. It is a total waste of money!

Internet

234. Slow down your internet service. You might be paying for more speed than you need.

235. Check if you qualify for a subsidy. Many state governments and providers subsidize internet service to make it more affordable. If you make less than $35,000.00 per year, you might be able to get internet for $9.95 per month. Visit EveryoneOn.org to check if you qualify.

236. Negotiate. If you have more than one internet service provider in your area, you have leverage because you can threaten to switch.

237. Hire a third party to negotiate for you. Try BillFixers.com. They will argue down the rates for you but keep half of your savings.

238. Cancel your internet service. I know some people who canceled their internet service and only used internet at the public library or local cafe.

Cable

239. Buy your own cable modem. Internet service providers charge an extra $8.00 to $10.00 per month to use their modem. It is a lease that never ends.

240. Cancel your cable bill. In 2016, the average cable bill was $103.00 per month. You can live without cable. The last time I watched television on a regular basis was thirteen years ago. Also, if you call and threaten to cancel, sometimes they will give you a big discount to keep you.

241. Buy a good HDTV antenna. If you want to cancel your cable, but you still want access to major networks, buy the 1byone Amplified HDTV Antenna for $29.99 on Amazon. Many customer reviews for that product said it saved them a lot of money.

242. Buy a streaming media player. Buy a media player such as Amazon Fire TV, Android TV, Apple TV, Google Chromecast, or Roku. Then subscribe to the streaming service you want: Netflix, Amazon Instant Video, Hulu, Showtime, HBO Now, Starz, CBS All Access, etc. For most people, one or two streaming services are sufficient. Opting for this method slashes your cable bill in half.

Chapter 7

Food

Groceries

243. Cook from scratch. The American view of cooking is skewed. My professor, Dr. Shi, said that when she first came to America from China, she lived with a college roommate. One day, Dr. Shi saw her roommate in the kitchen and asked, "What are you doing?" The roommate responded, "I'm cooking." Dr. Shi was confused when she did not see any ingredients on the kitchen counter or any pots and pans on the stove. When she asked for clarification, the roommate said, "I'm microwaving my frozen dinner." Folks, that is not cooking. In Chinese culture, this behavior is considered bizarre. Also, frozen and prepackaged meals are far more expensive than the raw ingredients used in them. They are also extremely unhealthy because they are loaded with salt, calories, and preservatives. Learn to cook fresh food.

244. Change your job. People who work long hours do not have time to cook from scratch. My friend Michele works as a CPA, and she typically works from 9:00 AM to 7:00 PM during busy seasons. Since Michele is glued to her desk all day, she does not have time to cook. She has been trying to lose weight and pays at least $725.00 per month for Jenny Craig food. This is very expensive and the food is not very good. Her grocery bill is four times higher than mine. At least she can afford it with her salary.

245. Create a window garden. You can grow your own fruits and vegetables in your apartment or house so long as you have a window that gets direct sunlight. NPR did a story on this. It is called window farming, and you can make your own hydroponic gardening system for only $30.00.

246. Buy whole foods. Healthy food is not expensive. My husband and I buy whole foods and cook from scratch. Our grocery bill for the two of us is around $350.00 per month, which is $175.00 per person. According to the USDA Grocery Budget Guidelines, we fall into the Thrifty Food Plan. If you fall into the Low-Cost Food Plan category, you are doing well compared to the average American.

247. Use everything you have. Use all produce before they spoil. Use all canned foods before buying more. The largest component of solid municipal waste in the United States is rotten food. Please do not let any food go to waste. Use SuperCook.com and MyFridgeFood.com to search for recipes based on the ingredients you already have. Or you can shop with recipes already planned out for the week, so you never end up wasting food.

248. Be aware of when you are full. American portion sizes are way too large. Chew your food thoroughly and take your time to eat. It takes 20 minutes for your brain to register that your stomach is full. By eating less, you save money and keep obesity at bay.

249. Eat leftovers. I am against the idea of cleaning your plate because it encourages you to overeat after you already feel full. Instead, store your leftovers in the refrigerator and then reheat another day. You can also find a creative way to reuse your leftovers in another recipe. I know people who toss their leftovers in the trash because they hate the taste of reheated food. Do not let food go to waste.

250. Cancel meal subscriptions. The most popular meal subscriptions are Blue Apron, Hello Fresh, Plated, and Home Chef. These companies deliver pre-portioned meal ingredients and recipes. They remove the need for grocery shopping, meal planning, and meal prepping. Blue Apron charges $59.99 per week for three meals, two servings each. That costs around $9.99 per meal. While it is cheaper than eating at a restaurant, it is still expensive. With $60.00, you can buy an entire week's worth of groceries for a single person. It is cheaper to buy the raw ingredients at the grocery store and cook the same exact recipes at home. You end up with enough leftovers for lunch the next day and enough ingredients to use in other meals.

251. Stop buying organic. Organic food is overrated. Buy fresh produce but forget about this whole overrated organic hype that is taking place across the United States. The first time my husband and I went grocery shopping after pooling our income, he bought organic butter for $5.24, which was ridiculously overpriced. It was too bad I didn't notice it was organic until we were checking out. Just stop! Regular butter is just as good as organic butter.

252. Substitute ingredients. Some recipes use expensive ingredients or call for ingredients you do not normally use and may therefore go to waste. Substitute using cheaper ingredients or find ways to use the ingredients you already have.

253. Become a vegetarian or eat less meat. Meat is expensive. Compared to meat-eaters, vegetarians save at least $750.00 per year.

254. Preserve sliced bread in the freezer. Frozen sliced bread can be put in the toaster right away. This is a good idea for single people who do not finish their bread fast enough.

255. Eat legumes. There are so many different types of beans you can eat: adzuki beans, black beans, soybeans, Anasazi beans, fava beans, garbanzo beans, kidney beans, lima beans, lentils, green peas, snow peas, snap peas, split peas, and black-eyed peas. Legumes are extremely cheap and healthy. They are packed with nutrients and fiber, which means you feel full after eating a small portion.

256. Boil dried beans. Canned beans cost on average $0.60 per cup. On the other hand, cooking your own dried beans cost on average $0.25 per cup. Canned beans are more than twice the price of dried beans. Soak the dried beans for eight hours either overnight or before you leave for work in the morning. Also, if you think beans take too much time to cook, then cook a large batch and refrigerate in mason jars. That way, you have cooked beans available for weeknights.

257. Weigh the 5 lbs. bag of onions or potatoes before buying. It is impossible to fill a bag with exactly 5 lbs. of onions or potatoes. Sometimes, it weighs more. Sometimes, it weighs less. The price is the same, regardless. Back when I ate potatoes every week, I weighed a couple bags on the scale before buying. Sometimes I got a 6 lbs. bag of potatoes, which meant I got more for my money.

258. Forage for food in the woods. Become a hunter-gatherer like your ancestors. Be careful not to eat any poisonous berries!

259. Buy produce that is in season. Seasonal produce is cheap because it is abundant and requires less time and labor to produce. Visit USDA.gov to see which fruits and vegetables are in season right now.

260. Freeze produce. Learn how to freeze produce properly. When you cannot finish all the produce in your refrigerator, freeze them and use them later. Do not let food go to waste.

261. Drink tap water. Tap water is the cheapest drink out there. Beverages such as soda, tea, milk, juice, coffee, beer, and wine are much more expensive than tap water.

262. Buy premade fruit juice instead of juicing fruits at home. It is cheaper to buy fruit juice because fresh fruit is expensive. Manufacturers use fruit pieces that are not aesthetically attractive—think of ugly, bruised fruits bitten by birds and insects—since nobody can tell how they look after being peeled and pulverized. Unless you own a fruit tree, it is not cost effective to make your own juice.

263. Keep a supply of powdered milk. When you run out of fresh milk, use the powdered milk until your next trip to the grocery store. Avoid buying overpriced milk at your nearby convenience store.

264. Consider dairy alternatives. Consider buying almond milk, coconut milk, flax milk, hemp milk, rice milk, and soy milk in addition to cow milk. When you are flexible and open to drinking dairy alternatives, you save money by buying whichever is on sale now.

265. Buy large containers of plain yogurt. It is cheaper than buying single-serving containers. Add your own toppings to plain yogurt because the flavored varieties found in stores contain sugar and unsafe additives. This is the cheapest way to eat yogurt.

266. Read seafood labels. When you find seafood products that are labeled as "previously frozen," they are not fresh. If that is the case, you might as well walk to the frozen food section and buy frozen seafood instead. Thaw it yourself. It costs 40 percent less.

267. Buy whole chickens. After using the meat, use the bones for chicken stock.

268. Use refried beans in tacos. Ground beef is expensive, so using refried beans along with ground beef will stretch the ground beef even further. Make the refried beans yourself from dried beans.

269. Eat roadkill cuisine. Vickie and John on *Extreme Cheapskates* search for roadkill instead of buying meat from the grocery store. In that episode, they found a rabbit carcass along the road and then served it as a meal for their guests.

270. Keep packets of condiments from fast-food restaurants. You can always use the extra ketchup, mustard, and mayonnaise later.

271. Avoid vending machines. Vending machines are horribly overpriced. Buy your snacks and beverages at the grocery store instead.

Supermarkets

272. Make a grocery list. A grocery list prevents impulsive buying. Make a list and stick to it. Order your grocery items based on where they are in the store. This way, you get in and out of the grocery store as fast as possible. The longer you stay, the more you buy.

273. Keep a running list of items you have run out of. Throughout the week, write a list of the grocery foods and household products you have run out of. Hang the list on your refrigerator door. When you make your grocery list, remember to include those items. Doing this helps you avoid making multiple trips to the grocery store, so you save money on transportation.

274. Shop for groceries on a full stomach. You spend more when you shop on an empty stomach. Suddenly, all the cakes and cookies look irresistible, and it is hard to focus on sticking to your grocery list.

275. Design your meal plan around the weekly flyer. Retale is a smartphone app that gives you all the digital weekly flyers in your area. Look through the flyers, take note of the sales, and make a list of the ingredients you already have in your refrigerator and pantry. Then plan five recipes based on what is on sale. You will effortlessly save money by never paying full price for most of your ingredients.

276. Only buy the amount you need. Supermarkets like to price their food products a certain way to gain more profit. For instance, buy 10 yogurts for $10.00. This kind of pricing is a gimmick. Since I used to work as a cashier at a supermarket, I saw how most people fell for these pricing gimmicks. Almost all the customers bought 10 yogurts. You can buy 3 yogurts and still get them for $1.00 each. You save money by only buying the amount you need.

277. Make a price book. Supermarket grocery prices are always shifting. How do you know for certain whether an advertised special is a good deal? Make a price book. Track the price variations of the grocery items you normally buy and include different supermarkets too. This way, you know which supermarket has the best price for a certain item and when. Keep it simple by using a spiral notebook or an Excel spreadsheet.

278. Avoid clipping coupons for groceries. Most coupons exist to increase demand for products you do not need. Almost all coupons are for unhealthy junk food. I have watched *Extreme*

Couponers. Quite frankly, I am absolutely amazed by how customers can buy $600.00 worth of groceries for less than $5.00 after ringing up coupons. If you look at their stockpile though, it is filled with boxes of processed foods. How often will you find a coupon for apples? Never. You save money now with coupons, but you pay more in medical bills in the future.

279. Get cash back with Ibotta. Ibotta is a free smartphone application that rewards cash back on groceries you were already buying anyway. Look through the deals, unlock them, scan your receipt, and then scan the barcodes on your groceries. Within 24 hours, Ibotta credits your account. Ibotta only allows you to withdraw your cash back money after reaching the $20.00 minimum, though. It took me three weeks to earn $20.50. I realized after signing up that I could have made more money by joining a team.

280. Bring your own canvas bags when shopping for groceries. I use the same three canvas bags every time I go grocery shopping. I use three canvas bags instead of 10 plastic bags. I like the fact that they are durable and reusable, limiting the number of plastic bags that end up littering the ocean. At some supermarkets like Market Street and Sprouts in Lubbock, I got a $0.05 discount for every reusable bag.

281. Skip the candy and cookies aisle. These processed junk foods add no nutritional value to your diet.

282. Buy store brand. My friend Yuwei loves to cook, but she is sensitive to price when shopping for groceries. She memorizes prices. Whenever her fiancé picks up a name-brand item, she tells him to put it back and get the store-brand version. Yuwei says that a dollar here and a dollar there is not much but buying store brand saves her $20.00 on each grocery trip. The money adds up.

283. Compare unit prices. Knowing the unit price can help you choose between two brands. It can also help you choose between two sizes. Sometimes, you calculate the unit price yourself. Oftentimes, the left side of the price tag displays the unit price.

284. Stock up on sale items that you use often. Be sure to only buy items that you use. Do not buy grocery items simply because they are on sale. When I worked at ShopRite, customers with children bought 10 of everything whenever something was on sale. It was a good idea to stock up even though they weren't going to use everything in the same week because they were going to finish it all eventually. When stocking up, remember to check the expiration dates before buying.

285. Ask for a rain check. When grocery items that are on sale go out of stock, go to the customer service counter and ask for a rain check. After the store restocks the items and the sale is already over, you can use your rain check to buy those items at the sale price.

286. Use the smallest wheeled cart you can find. Large shopping carts make customers buy more food, as the carts can fit more grocery items. The handheld baskets are not good either. Customers carrying handheld baskets were more likely to buy candy and soda as an unconscious reward for straining to carry the basket (Tuttle, 2011). Get the smaller shopping cart if your supermarket offers two sizes (Jacobs, 2017).

287. Create your own playlist for grocery shopping. Stores encourage customers to move slowly through the aisles by playing music with a slower beat. Customers who move at a slower pace purchase 29 percent more. This is a manipulative technique. Combat this by creating a playlist of upbeat songs.

288. Look on the higher and lower shelves. Supermarkets place the more expensive brands at eye level, which are usually on the middle shelves. The least expensive brands tend to be on the very top and bottom shelves.

289. Look for the clearance aisle. Many supermarkets have a clearance or promotional aisle that contains all the grocery items that are currently on sale You can also look for day-old baked goods or dented cans.

290. Keep your eyes on the cash register monitor. As a former cashier at ShopRite, it was very easy for me to ring up items twice by accident, especially when there were long lines, and everyone felt pressured to work faster. Sometimes items rang up at the wrong price, but these situations were hard to catch, as prices changed every week. Many customers with orders totaling over $200.00 almost never caught the double scanning or mispricing errors because they had so much stuff. Do not let this be you. Either keep your eyes on the cash register monitor as the cashier rings up your purchase or examine your receipt afterward. My mom always counts the number of items in her basket and compares it to the number on the receipt before she leaves the store.

291. Get your bottle deposit refund. Get $0.05 back for every bottle that you return to the store. In New York City, people make a living by scrounging through plastic recycling bins for bottles. They collect bags upon bags of bottles and return them for a refund.

292. Sign up for a membership card at your supermarket. Customers can sign up for free membership cards at many supermarkets. They can use these cards to get special discounts or rack up reward points. From October to November at the ShopRite where I used to work, customers who purchased $400.00 worth of groceries and merchandise receive a free frozen turkey for Thanksgiving.

293. Price match at Walmart or Target. Look through ads from local grocery stores and then make a list of the best deals. It must be an identical item, meaning same brand, make, model, size, color, etc. in order for Walmart or Target to match the lower price.

294. Split your Costco membership with someone. Costco is great for buying in bulk. A Costco membership costs $60.00 per year, and each membership comes with two cards. Supposedly, the second card is for a household member, but since they never check, you can split it with a friend or relative.

295. Compare supermarket prices to drug store prices on groceries. Drug store grocery items are wildly overpriced, but the weekly deals on certain items could be a steal. I remember buying a dozen eggs for $1.00 at Walgreens a few years ago. Also, supermarket guru, Phil Lempert, says that milk is one item you might want to buy at the drug store instead, depending on which part of the country you are in.

296. Shop at your local ethnic market. The prices are significantly lower. My parents shop at Asian supermarkets exclusively, and I notice that the prices for produce are always lower compared to American supermarkets. The prices might be lower because Asian communities rely on fresh produce diets and buy more produce to offset the lower profit margins.

297. Shop at discount grocery stores. The supply is limited, but the low prices are worth it. Stock up whenever you find grocery items with the lowest price in town.

298. Shop at warehouse clubs. Prices at Costco, BJ's, and Sam's Club are generally 30 percent lower than you would find at large supermarket chains. However, only buy what you need there, and shop for the rest at the supermarket. It is easy to justify spending a lot of money on bulk items (e.g., chocolate chip cookies and potato chips) to offset the annual membership fee. Some members spend $500.00 per trip at Costco and still come home with nothing substantial to eat for dinner.

299. Shop at farmers markets. Depending on which part of the country you live in, produce, meat and dairy might be cheaper at the farmers market. In New York City, the prices are much higher than at the grocery store. It depends on which grocery store and which items you are comparing farmers market prices to. This article is 2 years old, but hey, two years ago you could buy produce for less money at the farmers market than at the grocery store in Massachusetts (Norton, 2018). Not sure about now since things change, so do your research before shopping at your local grocery store.

300. Negotiate at farmers markets. When you become a regular customer, you have more power to negotiate. Also, try coming when the market is about to close. At that point, the farmers just want everything gone.

301. Buy specialty food items online. For items that are not commonly stocked by grocery stores, buy on Amazon. You can find specialty food items at health food stores, but they are very expensive.

302. Dumpster dive for discarded food. Grocery stores throw away fresh foods that are still edible. Too much food goes to waste. Research the anti-consumerist movement called freeganism. Also, if you live in New York City or any other urban area, you can dumpster dive with other people on certain nights of the week. Visit Meetup.com to find your local dumpster diving meetup group.

303. Quit shopping at whole foods. Whole Foods should be renamed "Whole Paycheck." Whole Foods is so overpriced that I have no idea how people in New York City can even afford shopping there. All the customers must be rich or something. My ex-boyfriend Jared (name changed to protect the implicated) always bought his honey from Whole Foods because he believed it was higher quality. Manuka Honey at Whole Foods costs $79.99 for 500 grams! He bought a cheaper one, but really? How can you justify the prices there? It must be excellent marketing or maybe the carefully made packaging leading customers to falsely believe that everything is healthy and natural.

Kitchen Appliances and Supplies

304. Buy a Vitamix-certified reconditioned standard blender. Vitamix is the way to go. The blenders are better than any standard blender you can pick up at Walmart. The Vitamix Certified Reconditioned Standard Blender works like new but costs $150.00 cheaper than a new one. Buy the extended warranty for $75.00, so then Vitamix will repair your machine for the next eight years.

305. Invest in a CrockPot and use it. Forget about ordering takeout on nights when you feel too tired to cook after getting home from work. Get a CrockPot. CrockPots make cooking simple, easy, and hassle-free. Before you head to work, prep your ingredients, put them in your CrockPot, and let the meal cook on low heat for six to eight hours. With a CrockPot, there is no excuse not to cook from scratch, especially for people who work full-time.

306. Buy used copper pots and pans lined with stainless steel. Copper cookware warms quickly and distributes heat evenly. The stainless-steel lining makes it easy to clean and maintain. Unfortunately, manufacturers like to cut corners, and the copper cookware you are buying might be very thin, which means it is not durable and needs to be replaced eventually. I bought my used copper pots and pans on eBay. They were made in 1960, which means they are older than my mother! They were still in excellent condition when I received them.

307. Sharpen your kitchen knives. Instead of buying new kitchen knives, take care of your current ones to keep them working as good as new.

308. Use reusable cups, bowls, plates, and utensils. This one is obvious, but surprisingly, there are people who do not do this. I used to have two roommates who ate with disposable plastic dinnerware because they were too lazy to wash their own dishes. Total waste of money! Plus, eating with reusable dinnerware (ceramic, glass, steel) elevates the eating experience to a new level.

309. Use reusable sandwich and snack bags. Ziploc bags are a waste of money. Plus, reusable ones are extremely cute.

310. Use a reusable water bottle. Two-thirds of Americans do not drink enough water. Combat this by always carrying a reusable water bottle with you. Quit buying overpriced disposable bottles of water.

Make Your Own

311. Brew your own coffee at home. People pay a premium for the convenience of buying brewed coffee at a café. Compared to going to the local café on the way to work, you could save around $936.00 per year if you brew your own coffee at home five days per week.

312. Make your own croutons. Store-bought croutons are ridiculously overpriced. Making your own is so easy that you will never go back to buying them. Croutons are also a way of repurposing stale bread.

313. Make your own yogurt. Homemade yogurt is much cheaper than store-bought yogurt.

314. Make your own nut butter. Store-bought nut butter is filled with sugar, salt, and hydrogenated oils. Homemade nut butter is much cheaper, tastier, and healthier than store-bought nut butter. The Vitamix blender can grind nuts to a very smooth consistency. Once you've made your own nut butter, you will never go back.

315. Make your own hummus. Store-bought hummus is expensive. You can make it yourself using dried chickpeas, tahini, a bunch of other cheap ingredients, and a Vitamix blender. Using canned chickpeas will increase the cost dramatically.

316. Make your own whipped cream. Store-bought whipped cream is full of additives and preservatives. It is also twice the price of homemade whipped cream, plus homemade is a billion times tastier.

317. Bake your own bread. Fresh homemade bread is cheaper, tastier, and more nutritious than store-bought bread filled with preservatives. Homemade bread is not cheaper than the cheapest store-brand loaf of white bread, but it is cheaper than most brands.

318. Make your own vanilla extract. As someone who loves to bake, I am constantly put off by the price of store-bought vanilla extract. A small bottle of vanilla extract is just too expensive, and it is not even the best quality. Buy Grade B Madagascar vanilla bean pods online, as the prices are lower than what you'll find in the grocery store. As for the alcohol, do not buy premium liquor, as the quality is not as important as the vanilla beans. Buy flavorless grain alcohol.

319. Make your own vinegar. Vinegar is cheap and easy to make. It just involves weeks to months of waiting time to make it from scratch, which is why most people buy it instead.

320. Grind your own grain. Grinding your own grain is cheaper only if you are an avid baker who uses a lot of flour. Buy a quality grain mill and buy unground whole grains online in bulk, as in 50 pounds per order. Whole grains can stay fresh for years.

321. Slice and dice your own food. Prepackaged sliced and diced food is expensive compared to buying the uncut version and cutting it at home. For instance, a package of cut and cored pineapple costs $5.99, while an uncut pineapple costs $3.99.

322. Make your own asparagus water. A Whole Foods store in Los Angeles sold asparagus water for $5.99. Seriously, if you want asparagus water, buy a pound of asparagus at Whole Foods for $4.99 and make it yourself. Stick three stalks of asparagus into a container of water and voila.

323. Bring your own lunch to work. One day a week, prepare all your lunch meals for the rest of the week. Keep it simple by making sandwiches, salads, or CrockPot meals. Wrap the sandwiches or store your salads and CrockPot meals in smaller containers. I like using Mason jars because they are airtight and easy to stack. Another option is to eat last night's leftovers for today's lunch. Before you head to work in the morning, grab what you need, put it into your lunch bag, and go. With this, you never order takeout for lunch at $10.00 a day ever again. The only time it does not make sense to bring your own lunch is when your company offers cafeteria food for free or for a low price. At the Overton Hotel where I used to work, each meal was only $2.00, so it never made sense to bring my own food.

Recipes

324. Make recipes from 5DollarDinners.com. Erin Chase from $5 Dinners started couponing in 2008 and always challenged herself to make dinner meals that cost under $5.00. She shares these recipes on her website, and all the prices are accurate. However, she buys food that is on sale or with a coupon. Also, prices vary by region in the United States.

325. Make recipes from BudgetBytes.com. Beth Moncel from Budget Bytes is broke, but she loves eating delicious, quality foods. On her website, she shares recipes that are simple, quick, and satisfying to make. All recipes are catered toward people who have tight food budgets.

326. Make recipes from The99CentChef.blogspot.com. Billy Vasquez from the 99 Cent Chef makes recipes from ingredients that cost $0.99 or less. He loves shopping from 99¢ Only Stores.

327. Make recipes from BrokeAssGourmet.com. Gabi Moskowitz from BrokeAss Gourmet makes gourmet meals for under $20.00.

328. Make recipes from NotEatingOutInNY.com. Cathy Erway from Not Eating Out In New York only ate food that she cooked herself from 2006 to 2008. She has tried it all: diving into dumpsters, foraging, cooking for groups, and competing in amateur contests. The cost for one serving of each dish she makes rarely exceeds $5.00. Considering that she lives in New York City, that is not bad at all.

329. Make recipes from TheStoneSoup.com. Jules Clancy from the Stone Soup shares recipes that contain only five ingredients and take only 10 minutes to make. Jules eats a low-carb diet because she has type 2 diabetes.

330. Make recipes from WellPlated.com. Erin Clarke from Well Plated shares healthy and delicious recipes that anyone can make on a weeknight. A lot of people cannot be bothered with cooking because they think cooking takes too much time. While Erin's recipes are not the cheapest out there, they have short prep times. Cooking quick, healthy meals at home is still cheaper than dining out.

Restaurants

331. Eat with people who can do basic arithmetic. For some reason, when dining with a group at a restaurant, there is always one person who throws in $20.00 for a $19.00 meal, feigning ignorance to the fact that it is not enough to cover the tip. Then there is something that I personally call "the uneven even split." For example, a group of drinkers wants to split the bill evenly with the person who only drank water. One time, I went to a karaoke joint for my friend Qwency's farewell party. I had to leave early and wanted to pay for my fair share, but the group told me not to pay—they would tell me how much I owed the next day. The next day they told me I owed $25.00. I was only there for two hours, drank only water, and ate from the shared plate of chicken! How on earth was the bill that expensive? As it turned out, the group ordered a ton of beer after I left and then decided to split the bill evenly with me, someone who only drank water. I was pissed. Even splits are uneven and unfair. Today I am wary of group invitations.

332. Check the restaurant before you go. Check the menu prices online before you say yes. One time, an online meetup group invited me to a café. I figured bringing only $7.00 in cash was enough, as I planned on only drinking hot cocoa. When I got there, I was told that there was a prix fixe brunch until 4:00 P.M. for $18.00 (more like $22.29 after tax and tip). Although I already ate lunch, I was forced to order the brunch that I didn't even have the money to pay for. I am lucky and thankful that my friend Chelsea paid for my meal. However, had I known, I would not have gone in the first place.

333. Order water. Coffees, teas, sodas, juices, and alcoholic beverages are overpriced. The profit margin on food is not that high, but it is on drinks.

334. Skip the appetizer. Oftentimes, I am full enough with only an entrée. If an entrée is not enough for you, then eat a light snack before you go. By the way, some restaurants offer free bread or chips and salsa. At Chinese restaurants, expect to get salted peanuts. Servers often bring these out after you order to ensure you buy an appetizer. Check on Yelp before you go to know whether the restaurant offers free bread and butter.

335. Skip dessert. Like drinks, desserts are also overpriced. If you want dessert, eat dessert after you get home. I admit I do order dessert if I cannot buy it myself at the grocery store or bakery. For instance, I would order Japanese mochi ice cream, as I could only buy it at one oriental grocery store in Lubbock, TX, and it was quite far.

336. Split your meal. Portion sizes in America are gigantic. If you and a friend can feel full by sharing an entrée and an extra side salad, then do it. Be sure to still tip the server well.

337. Save half of your meal for later. I can never finish an entire plate or bowl from a restaurant. I usually ask for a doggy bag and take my leftovers home with me to eat later. Sometimes I ask for a doggy bag in the very beginning and put half my food inside to avoid contamination with my saliva.

338. Get it to go. At some restaurants, you can order your food to go instead of dining in. My friend SoJin and I ordered our ramen noodles to go and then ate at our friend Phoebe's house. It was delicious, and it felt nice eating in the comfort of her home. We saved money by not having to tip. You can still tip a few dollars, but you do not need to tip the full 20 percent.

339. Pick up instead of requesting delivery. Some restaurants offer free delivery, but you still must tip the delivery person. My dad used to deliver food. There are some people who feign ignorance so they can avoid paying a tip for delivery. Do not be that cheap. Delivery people make around $3.00 an hour and make the rest of their wages from tips. The alternative to delivery is picking up, which is inconvenient but free, well... except for gas, unless you walk!

340. Avoid dining at restaurants on major holidays. On major holidays, restaurants are extremely crowded. Some restaurants even create a prix fixe menu specifically for major holidays. Sure, you can get a three-course meal for $49.00 per person. But what if you want an entrée that is only $15.00? Celebrate by dining the day before or the day after. You get the food you want without paying too much.

341. Order from the kid's menu. Kids meals are good for quick and light lunches, and they are also cheaper.

342. Eat at a buffet. For all-you-eat, buffets are quite affordable. It depends on your geographic location, though. While a buffet in New York City costs $15.00 or more per person, a buffet in Lubbock costs only $9.00 per person. Another reason to eat at a buffet is that it makes the billing process easy for groups (See #331).

343. Go out for lunch. Lunch is cheaper than dinner.

344. Eat at fast-casual restaurants. At places like Chipotle, Five Guys, Panera Bread, Pei Wei, etc., you are not expected to tip. You can get great food without having to tip 15 percent or more.

345. Stop buying fast food. Fast food is cheap but cooking the same thing at home is even cheaper.

346. Get a birthday discount. Some restaurants let the birthday person eat for free.

347. Use Groupon.com. Groupon.com has steep discounts. Just be sure to tip the server based on the bill's original total and not the discounted total.

348. Use the discount at the bottom of your receipt. At some franchises, there is a link to complete a survey found at the bottom of the receipt. Complete the survey, and you get free food on your next meal.

349. Eat samples at Costco. You can get full after eating all the delicious samples.

350. Go during Happy Hour. In addition to half-price drink specials during Happy Hour, some restaurants give discounts on food too. The food usually has smaller portions.

351. Bring your own. Breweries that do not serve food usually let customers bring their own food. Restaurants that do not serve alcohol sometimes have a BYOB policy.

352. Avoid sports bars. Buy snacks from the grocery store and watch sports at home. You eat mindlessly when watching TV at a sports bar, and therefore you are not as mindful with your spending.

353. Drink alcoholic beverages at home. It is cheaper than going to the local bar.

354. Go on slow days. On certain days of the week, it is notoriously slow for restaurants. Restaurants usually offer specials to attract customers.

355. Eat at restaurants where children eat for free. On certain days of the week, restaurants let children eat for free to attract families. For instance, some Firehouse Subs franchises have Kids Eat Free nights.

Chapter 8

Clothing

Shopping Habits

356. Buy clothes directly from the manufacturer. During my vacation in Mexico, my friends Rod and Michelle took me to a Levi's jean factory. I bought a pair of Levi's retailing for $64.00 USD for only $9.00 USD. If the factory sold the jeans for $9.00 USD and still made a profit, imagine how little it costs to make a pair of Levi's.

357. Shop at sample sales. You can get an extremely good deal if you go early. My mom bought a down jacket for only $5.00. At a Kipling sample sale, she bought me a cross-body mini bag for under $20.00. I love the bag because it's pretty and practical. I wear it everywhere I go.

358. Avoid shopping at factory outlets. The clothes tend to be of low quality. Also, the clothing manufacturers made half of the clothes specifically for the factory outlet. Therefore, you are not actually saving the amount of money that outlet stores claim.

359. Buy clothes that are exempt from sales tax. In the following states, clothes are generally tax-exempt: Massachusetts, Minnesota, New Jersey, New York, Pennsylvania, Rhode Island, and Vermont. There are some restrictions. For example, in New York, only clothes under $110.00 are exempt. Try to buy clothes retailing at $109.99 or lower. If it retails at $110.00, you pay $119.76 after tax.

360. Borrow clothes and accessories when you only need it once. For semiformal or formal events, try borrowing from your friends or coworkers first. They might have something suitable in your size. After you are done, clean it and return it in the same condition you received it. Treat that person to dinner to say thanks.

361. Buy clothes you can pay for immediately, not on store charge cards. Charge cards encourage you to spend money you don't have on clothes you don't need. Also, some charge cards have annual fees and crazy APR.

362. Beware of clothing sales. Clothing sales are designed to suck you into buying clothes that you do not need. They give you an excuse to justify your spending habits. Buy clothes because you need them or already planned on buying them, not because they were on sale. For instance, my sister needed to buy a pair of white shoes for her graduation ceremony. Apparently, this was the mandatory dress code for all girls. We found a pair of white shoes for $50.00 at Nine West. The cashier asked me whether I wanted to buy a second pair for half off. Unless I already planned on buying shoes for myself in the first place, the answer is always no. Think of it like this. The second pair cost $50.00 originally and only $25.00 after the discount. By buying the second pair though, I did not save $25.00—I spent an extra $25.00 on something I did not originally intend on buying.

363. Shop strategically during clothing sales. For buy one, get one half off sales like the one mentioned above, find a friend who does want to buy a pair of shoes and then go together. Afterward, split the bill in half. For instance, you both bought a pair of shoes for $50.00, making the total bill $75.00 after the discount is applied. Split it even between the both of you by paying $37.50 per person. That way, you both save money.

364. Wait for holiday clothing sales. I can guarantee you that there will always be a big clothing sale whenever there is a holiday. If you need to buy clothes, wait until the next holiday. For instance, around the time I was almost finished with college, I needed to buy a three-piece suit. I wanted to be ready for any future job interviews. My friend Shani advised me to buy wool, as the fabric is breathable. Unfortunately, wool suits are twice the price of polyester. The tropical wool suit and separate blouse I wanted from Ann Taylor cost $384.57 in total. I wanted it since I was only going to buy one suit and it would be an investment for my future career. I waited until Black Friday and bought it for only $188.00! I paid half the original price.

365. Buy out-of-season clothing in the clearance section. Buy coats in the spring and bathing suits in the fall. Clothing retailers deeply discount the price to sell them fast and make space for new merchandise.

366. Discard your fashion magazines. Fashion magazines make you feel insecure. Eighty percent of women felt worse about themselves after looking through fashion magazines. The whole point is to make you feel bad and to think you need to buy certain clothes to feel good about yourself. The truth is, you get to decide how good you feel about yourself. Dump those magazines today.

367. Unsubscribe from apparel mailing lists. A lot of clothing retailers run flash sales to promote impulsive shopping. Customers believe that since the sale only lasts for one day, they better buy quickly. There are always sales! When I subscribed to Ann Taylor's mailing list, I received flash sale emails twice a week. They got annoying, so I unsubscribed. Ann Taylor and many other online retailers try too hard to make you part with your hard-earned money.

368. Say no when cashiers ask you for your phone number and email address. When I bought my sister the pair of white shoes from Nine West, I naively gave away my personal contact information. First, retailers put your phone number into a database and sell it to third parties for money. They already made money off you in the initial transaction, but those greedy corporations want to make even more. Second, they take your email address and add you to a mailing list without asking for permission first. Nine West did that and sent me nine emails per day about their promotions. No joke. Nine West desperately wanted me to part with my money. I clicked "unsubscribe," but it did not work. I emailed customer service and was told that I was already removed from the mailing list. That was not true because I kept getting emails. I had to set up a filter in my Gmail for emails containing the text "Nine West" to always go straight to spam. None of this would have happened had I just said no when the cashier asked me for my phone number and email address.

369. Avoid window shopping. Window shopping reminds you of all the money you do not have to buy things you do not need. Some window displays are so beautiful that you feel compelled to spend impulsively. Living in New York City, I often passed by Macy's on 34th Street and Herald Square. That department store had the most festive holiday windows ever. It made me want to go inside and shop. But nope, I just kept walking! In New York City, you've got places to go and people to see.

370. Check your clothes for imperfections before you buy. Check the fabric for holes, tears, buttons with frayed threads, sloppy stitching, loose stitching, stitches that don't lie flat, or spots that were stitched over multiple times. These are signs that indicate the clothes will fall apart after a few washes. Well-made garments are cut straight along the grain of the fabric, have interfacing where the structure is needed, and have binding on seams.

371. Ask for a discount if you see faulty zippers, missing buttons, or removable stains. Missing buttons and removable stains are easy to fix. Be careful with faulty zippers. Be certain that the garment will fit once the zipper is replaced. When I was shopping at Zara, I found an extremely cute dress with a faulty zipper. The cashier gave me a $5.00 discount, but it rendered the dress nonrefundable. I saved money, but unfortunately, when I took it home and replaced the zipper, I found out the dress was too small. There was no way for me to know this at the store because even though I tried it on, the faulty zipper prevented me from zipping it all the way up. I used my hands to close the gap, which made me think it would fit. Too bad it didn't.

372. Challenge yourself before buying new clothes. For instance, you can challenge yourself to think of three reasons to buy a new item of clothing. What three outfits in your wardrobe can you pair this item with?

373. Shop for clothes for the life you have now. Too many people do something called aspirational shopping. Many consumers, including me, get enticed by clothes and drift off into a fantasyland of how we would look great in (insert garment) once we (insert something that hasn't happened yet). Do not do that. For instance, do not buy jeans that will look great on you after going on a diet and losing 20 pounds. Buy jeans that fit you now.

374. Make a list of clothes you plan on buying and stick to it. This is just like shopping for groceries, except it applies to clothes. With a list, you don't get sidetracked into buying clothes you did not intend on buying.

375. Shop for secondhand clothes at thrift shops. I like buying secondhand clothes that are still in great condition. If the garment has been owned by someone else before, I know what it looks like after being washed. Nobody likes it when a perfectly new cotton shirt shrinks in the wash. I also know whether the clothes maintain their original shape after being worn.

376. Shop for secondhand clothes online. In the past, I bought almost all my clothes on eBay, and no one could ever tell. People always think I look well put together. Shopping on eBay can be trickier than at thrift shops. I like to narrow my search based on brand name and size. Ann Taylor is my favorite brand, but their clothes are too pricey for me. I like to buy them used on eBay. For instance, on eBay, I typically search "Ann Taylor Size 4 Dress." Sometimes I like to filter the results based on color and price range. I only consider listings that have lots of pictures, a detailed description of the condition, and an explanation of why it is being sold. I also compare the dress measurements to my body measurements. I make sure the dress measurements are slightly wider, so I could have some breathing ease when wearing it. For listings that let you submit an offer, I offer a price around $3.00 to $5.00 less. Most sellers agree to my offer. Lately, since ThredUp has become so popular and their customer service is great, I've been shopping secondhand on ThredUp exclusively. I like the ease of finding my favorite brands in my size and colors, and I get a good sense of how the clothes drape since they always use the same mannequin. I either put down a $10 deposit to get a favorites goody box and try 10 items, or I'll buy 10 items outright on a credit card, try the clothes on, and keep only the best, returning the rest for a refund before my credit card payment comes due. You can try PoshMark too as an option. A lot of people have had good experiences with PoshMark but I've read stories of sellers writing inaccurate descriptions and the return policy isn't good, so I haven't tried PoshMark for myself yet.

377. Buy generic basic clothes. Do not buy a basic t-shirt at Armani Exchange for $35.00 when you can buy the same thing at Target for $8.00.

378. Ask for discounts when shopping at boutiques. When purchasing multiple items at a boutique, ask whether you can get a discount. Also, try to see whether you can get a discount by offering to pay cash. You save the boutique from paying merchant processing fees.

Clothing Wardrobe

379. Build an all-season wardrobe. I save a lot of money by wearing the same dresses all year round. I still wear summer dresses in the winter. I keep my body warm by wearing sweaters and leggings. Another thing you can do is to buy some silk garments. Silk keeps you cool in the summer and warm in the winter.

380. Try the Project 333 fashion experiment. With this project, you can only wear 33 items of clothing, accessories, outerwear, and shoes combined. Underwear, sleepwear, loungewear, and workout clothes do not count. For the next three months, wear only those 33 items. When the experiment ends, and you find that you like it, adjust your wardrobe and do it again. For more information on Project 333, visit BeMoreWithLess.com.

381. Wear the same thing every day. In 2011, Kristy Powell from New Haven, CT wore the same little black dress for 365 days. She called this challenge, "The One Dress Protest." She had two identical dresses so she could wash one while wearing the other one. She kept her outfits looking unique by accessorizing. Kristy inspired me to cut down on my own wardrobe.

382. Create a work uniform. Steve Jobs wore the same thing to work every day: a black turtleneck and a pair of blue jeans. Mark Zuckerberg also does the same: a gray t-shirt, a hoodie, and a pair of blue jeans. An Australian TV anchor wore the same suit to work every day for a year, and no one noticed. Dave Ramsey wore the same blue dress shirt for each Financial Peace University video that he made, and I never noticed until my students pointed it out. I was surprised I never noticed because I watched his videos over 30 times before. It is work—no one cares what you wear as long as you produce great results (unless, of course, you are a celebrity and the media gossips about you).

383. Stick to classic and simple styles. Coco Chanel once said, "Fashion changes, but style endures." Look back through your photo albums from ten years ago. Some thoughts that might pop into your mind are, "What the heck was I wearing," or maybe, "Did I really use to wear that?" Create a classic wardrobe that you can wear for years instead of only this season. Do not waste money trying to stay trendy.

384. Buy clothes that make you look stunning. Having a wardrobe full of clothes but nothing to wear is, unfortunately, a common problem. Opt to buy fewer clothes, but only buy clothes that make you look and feel amazing. That way, you look and feel amazing, all day every day.

385. Buy clothes that can be machine-washed. Machine-washable, fancy clothes exist. Stay away from clothes that have "dry clean only" labels. The laundering costs add up quick.

386. Wear your clothes until they are completely worn out. If people followed this advice, they would still have their clothes for years. I tried doing this and realized that most people, including me, toss their clothes because they want to have a new look. People rarely toss their clothes due to being truly worn out. In 2014, my friend Chung gave me a replica Louis Vuitton wallet. Within a year, it started coming apart at the seams, especially the area where I stored my cash. I thought I would take it to its grave in a few weeks, but no. The wallet is three years old now, and I still have it. The seams never came apart further because I only stretched the wallet pocket to a certain point to get my cash.

387. Wear an apron when cooking and cleaning. Make your clothes last longer by not staining them.

388. Use fuzzy huggable hangers instead of plastic hangers. Fuzzy huggable hangers reduce shoulder distortion.

389. Hang your sweaters properly. Most people hang their sweaters like shirts, but since sweaters are heavy and stretchy, the shoulders get ruined. Make your sweaters last longer by hanging them properly. SnapGuide.com has instructions on how to hang a sweater.

390. Wear free t-shirts. This works if you work in the home improvement industry or something similar. When I used to work at a hardware store, all my coworkers wore free t-shirts. Their jobs involved touching dirty pipes and fittings, so it made sense to wear free t-shirts.

391. Wear convertible clothes. With convertible clothing, one garment can be worn in multiple styles. Some convertible garments can be worn as a dress, a skirt, a shirt, and as pants.

392. Buy high-quality winter coats. A good winter coat lasts a minimum of three years. I once saw a female customer at the grocery store wearing a fabulous trench coat. I complimented her on it, and she told me she bought it in 1970. Well-made coats can last for decades. Before buying your next coat, test the zippers to see whether the fabric gets caught in the zipper.

393. Invest in one high-quality swimsuit. When it comes to swimsuits, you get what you pay for. Cheap swimsuits are made of low-quality fabric and fit poorly. Too many women shop for new bikinis when the summer season rolls around. Instead, buy one expensive swimsuit that is made from good material, has strong seams, and fits you perfectly. A high-quality swimsuit will last for years. When shopping, stretch the swimsuit in multiple directions to see whether the seams break easily and whether white fabrics show. If either happens, do not buy it.

394. Avoid expensive workout clothing. For some reason, expensive workout clothing has become a status symbol. Why are women paying $400.00 for yoga pants? I bet Instagram celebrities played a role in popularizing expensive, overpriced workout clothing. Instagram users fawn over these hot models wearing workout clothes, and followers believe they can look just as good if they wore similar clothes. There is an entire industry capitalizing on America's obesity problem. Do not confuse fitness clothing with being physically fit. I only have two workout outfits (one for warm weather and one for cool weather). I paid $50.00 for everything at most.

395. Save your receipts when donating clothes to goodwill. Go through your closet and remove clothes that you no longer wear. This makes your closet more spacious. Either sell those clothes on eBay or donate them to Goodwill. Save the receipts from Goodwill, as you can claim a charitable deduction (if you itemize) when filing next year's tax return.

396. Make your own clothes. This tip only saves money if you like buying designer clothes. You just can't compare making your own clothes to ready-to-wear clothes from Walmart or Target. That's like comparing apples to oranges.

397. Host a clothing swap with your friends. One person's trash is another person's treasure. Your friends might like the clothes you no longer want and vice versa. To host a clothing swap, choose people to invite and make it a rule that everyone brings a set number of clothes or accessories to ensure fairness. State that all clothes must be clean and in good condition. On the day of the clothing swap, neatly arrange all the clothes. Let the party begin!

Shoes

398. Clean and condition your leather boots regularly. They last longer that way.

399. Rotate your shoes. Avoid wearing the same shoe for two or more consecutive days. If you wear the same pair every day, the shoe does not have enough time to dry and maintain its shape.

400. Wear identical black socks. Jacob Fisker from *Early Retirement Extreme* makes his socks last by wearing identical socks. They are easier to pair up after doing the laundry. Plus, when your socks disappear in the washing machine, you won't have mismatched socks. Why black? Many workplaces require black socks.

401. Use a mesh laundry bag when washing your socks. Never lose socks again!

402. Wear black or neutral-colored shoes. They are appropriate for any occasion, match with any outfit, and go well with black socks (See #400).

403. Own only one pair of boots, one pair of dressy shoes, one pair of sandals, and one pair of athletic shoes. I think women own way too many shoes. When I'm socializing, I'm not staring at people's shoes. I focus my attention on the face of the person I am speaking to. I only own one of each kind of shoe, which simplifies my decision-making. I choose which shoe to wear based on the weather. Jacob from *Early Retirement Extreme* recommends buying boots and dressy shoes in the same color, so you only need one color for shoe polish.

404. Buy high-quality, comfortable shoes. Stay away from cheap shoes. Not only do they make you look cheap, they only last one season. Instead of spending $30.00 each time to replace a pair of broken shoes, invest in a pair of high-quality shoes. They are well worth your money. Women, on average, own 20 pairs of shoes but wear only five. The number one reason is that the other shoes are too uncomfortable. In 2014, I bought a pair of New Balance sneakers for $68.00, and they are still in great condition. In 2016, I bought a pair of SoftWalk Jupiter Mary Jane shoes for $109.95. They still look new. Had I bought a cheap pair of Mary Jane shoes, they would have fallen apart by now.

405. Scrub shoes by hand instead of throwing them in the washing machine. Tossing shoes, especially canvas shoes, into the washing machine wears them out faster.

406. Clean and polish your shoes regularly. This extends the lifespan of your shoes.

407. Repair shoes instead of buying new. Take your shoes to a local cobbler for repair. When the straps on my Mary Jane shoes broke, I got them repaired for only $12.00. They are good as new.

408. Add a thin rubber sole to the bottom of new dress shoes. This protects the leather sole from damage. Rubber soles are also easier to replace than leather.

409. Protect your shoe soles with toe and heel taps. Toe and heel taps maintain the integrity of your soles. Without toe and heel taps, your soles deteriorate prematurely, which means you need to bring them in earlier for repair.

410. Use wooden shoe trees. Shoe trees help maintain the original shape of your shoes and absorb any moisture. When shoes absorb moisture, they do not last as long.

411. Avoid wearing high heels or wear them less often. High heels look sexy and stylish. They can be a real confidence booster. However, high heels can cause injuries to your foot, such as fractures, sprains, and strains. Save money by not having to see an osteopathic physician for injuries caused by high heels.

412. Avoid buying name-brand sneakers. Sneakers are no longer just athletic shoes—they are regarded as status symbols. Teenagers beg their parents to spend hundreds of dollars on a pair of Nikes. My friend Chung has a son who collects limited-edition sneakers and never wears them. Chung never says no to his son. It is ridiculous because his son never stops shopping for more sneakers. Just because Michael Jordan is a great basketball player who wears a pair of Nikes, doesn't mean you will become a great basketball player by wearing a pair of Nikes. NBA player Stephon Marbury embraces this very philosophy. He came out with his own line of sneakers that sell for less than $15.00. He wears the same sneakers when he is on the basketball court. A higher price does not equate to better performance. If the sneakers fit right, are comfortable, are durable, and are slip-resistant, they are good enough for exercise. Focus on practicing your sport and improving your performance instead of buying name-brand sneakers.

Accessories

413. Expand your wardrobe using accessories. Inexpensive accessories, such as necklaces, bracelets, earrings, rings, scarves, hats, and belts, make your wardrobe feel more exciting.

414. Buy a sturdy backpack. Cheap, fashionable backpacks break after a few weeks—a few months if you are lucky. Sturdy backpacks last longer, have smoother zippers and can be repaired. I bought an OGIO SoHo Women's Laptop Backpack for $69.00 in 2013. Four years later, it is still in excellent condition, and I plan on owning it for several more years to come. (See #32 for a story about the same backpack.)

415. Own one versatile and stylish handbag. I do this. I use the same Kipling cross-body mini bag everywhere I go. (See #357 for a story on how I got this bag for dirt cheap.) When this bag falls apart, I will buy another durable bag with zippered compartments and adjustable straps. I used to have more than one bag, but I just got sick of transferring items from one bag to another. Sometimes I forgot to bring something important because I left it in another bag. My friend Susan does the same. She has been using the same Medium Classic Leather AmeriBag for years ($149.59 on Amazon). She is a self-made millionaire who can afford anything she wants, but she has only one bag. Quit using designer handbags as status symbols.

416. Make a duct tape wallet. Trendy leather wallets cost over $40.00. With 15 minutes and three yards of duct tape, you can make your own wallet. It costs only $3.00 to make a simple mono-colored wallet. Apparently, duct tape wallets are durable too. My friend Jackie has been using the same duct tape wallet for the past four years!

417. Make waterproof tote bags out of broken umbrellas. Separate the umbrella fabric from the metal frame. All you need is a sewing machine, thread, scissors, and a smooth surface to cut on. DIYProjects.com has instructions on how to do this.

418. Buy a sturdy umbrella. One time, it was raining heavily, and I forgot to bring an umbrella. I bought a cheap umbrella for $4.50. The cheap umbrella was only good for three uses before saying hello to the trashcan. Cheap umbrellas are a waste of money. I personally use a Blunt™ Metro umbrella. I bought mine for $40.00 back when the company was new. All Blunt™ umbrellas come with a two-year warranty. Since my umbrella broke one month before the warranty expired, the company sent me another one for free. I owned the new one for two years already. I spent $40.00 on an umbrella and got four years of use out of it. Not bad!

419. Buy comfortable cotton underwear. Back in 2015, I designed a website for a makeup artist named ShuShu. In exchange, I wanted ShuShu to help me design a new wardrobe. Every time I changed in the dressing room, ShuShu pointed out that my panties weren't feminine enough. Quite frankly, I was single at the time and didn't give a damn about my underwear. What was the point if no one saw me naked anyway? She insisted on me buying lacey, sexy panties. I listened to her and bought an entire week's worth of nonrefundable panties. That was the worst purchase I made in my entire life. The panties were tight, itchy, and unbreathable, gave me constant wedgies, and gave me yeast infections. Ladies and gentlemen, buy comfortable underwear.

420. Go bra-free. Bras are absurdly overpriced. Bras contribute to back and shoulder pain and hinder lymphatic flow. Also, you might not know this—bras speed up the sagging process, as connective tissue in the breasts become weak from never being used. I used to have chest and shoulder pain after coming home from school. The pain disappeared after doing yoga but came back the next day. I soon realized that my bra caused pain. I stopped wearing underwire bras when I was 16 years old and never looked back. I do wear a sports bra when exercising though.

Alterations and Repairs

421. Tailor your clothes. Ready-to-wear clothes purchased off the rack never fit perfectly. There is always an area that's too wide, too tight, or too long. Altering your clothes can make you look like you're worth a million bucks. When I bought my secondhand cashmere sweaters on eBay, they did not fit perfectly. One was too long, and the other was too loose. I tailored them, and now they look amazing on me.

422. Learn to sew. If you know how to alter and repair clothing, then you do not need to pay a tailor to do it for you.

423. Cut your long jeans into shorts. When your jeans have holes or the hem is torn beyond repair, you can cut them into shorts. WikiHow.com has a tutorial on how to turn jeans into shorts. The result is very cute and fashionable.

424. Hem pants to the correct length. Your pants should not be touching the floor. If they are too long, they will wear out from being dragged across the floor. Ladies, if you switch between flats and high heels often, try using Hem Gems to temporarily adjust the pant length.

425. Repair your clothes. You can easily learn on your own how to stitch a button, mend a tear, and fix a hem. All you need are a needle, a spool of thread, and a pair of scissors. No need to go to the tailor for basic repairs.

426. Save the extra buttons that come with your new clothes. You never know when you might need them.

427. Replace your buttons strategically. For instance, my husband's jacket was missing a black button in the front. I could not find matching buttons at my local fabric shop. I did not want to pay $10.00 to replace all the buttons. Instead, I removed a button from the jacket sleeve and sewed it onto the front of the jacket. Then, I took a black button of the same size and sewed it on the sleeve. The button only cost $0.75, so I saved time and money.

428. Use binder clips for shorts that are too wide. Kate Hashimoto on *Extreme Cheapskates* bought a pair of shorts that were on sale. They were too wide at the waist, so she used a binder clip as a belt. She has been wearing those shorts for the past 13 years.

429. Dye faded fabrics. If your favorite t-shirt or pair of jeans faded in color, bring it back to life with fabric dye. This only works on natural fibers like cotton, linens, silk, ramie, and wool, and on synthetic fibers like nylon and rayon. Follow the instructions found on the fabric dye packaging.

Laundry

430. Wear your clothes more than once. Unless you sweat in or stain your clothes, you can wear most clothes at least twice before needing to wash them. Laundering too often shortens the lifespan of your clothes anyway. After wearing your clothes, hang them to air them out. Do not do this for underwear or socks—throw them in the wash.

431. Do your own laundry. Growing up, my mom always washed the laundry and then let me fold clothes for an allowance. I was shocked to find out that you can pay for "wash-and-fold" laundry service. Compared to doing it yourself at a coin-operated laundromat, using laundry service costs twice as much.

432. Wash your clothes using a breathing mobile washer and a 5-gallon bucket. The Breathing Mobile Washer is a product that looks like a toilet plunger, except it's for washing clothes, not for unclogging toilets. You can buy one on Amazon for $20.95. I used to manually wash my clothes using this product and saved water, electricity, detergent, and money.

433. Wash a full load of laundry. A full load of laundry uses the same amount of water and electricity as a partial load.

434. Zip your zippers before doing the laundry. This is to avoid tearing your garments while they are in the wash.

435. Wash your clothes with like colors. Some people (ahem, my husband) throw all their clothes into the washing machine without sorting first. Please take the time to sort. If you wash a red shirt and a pair of white pants together, you get pink pants. Unless you want to waste more time and money shopping for new clothes, sort the clothes first.

436. Wash your clothes in cold water. The clothes get just as clean as hot water while using less energy and money. Washing with hot water and rinsing with warm water costs $0.68 per load. Meanwhile, washing with cold water and rinsing with cold water costs $0.04 per load. You save $0.64 per load.

437. Make your own detergent. DIYNatural.com has a simple recipe for homemade detergent, which uses grated bar soap, borax, and washing soda. While Tide detergent costs $0.21 per load, homemade detergent only costs $0.05 per load.

438. Buy generic detergent. If you do not want to make your own detergent, then buy generic detergent. Generic detergent costs half the price of Tide.

439. Use less detergent. Detergent manufacturers recommend too much soap per load as a method for increasing sales. Go easy on the soap. You can use as little as one-eighth of the recommended amount. A little goes a long way, especially since modern washing machines have increased efficiency and use less water.

440. Use vinegar as a softener. White, distilled vinegar is hypoallergenic and works just as well as normal fabric softener while costing less. Every washing machine is different. Start with a 1/4 cup of vinegar at first and see how soft the clothes turn out. If more is needed, experiment by using between 1/2 cup and 1 cup of vinegar in the future.

441. Line-dry your clothes. You can save $120.00 per year in electric bills by line-drying your clothes. Plus, the clothes last longer.

442. Wring your clothes before line-drying. Invest in a clothes wringer. A clothes wringer can remove up to 90 percent of the water from your clothes. This speeds up the drying time, especially for wet towels that could take days to dry. A new one costs between $130.00 and $150.00.

443. Remove dryer lint from the machine before every use. Keeping the lint filter clean keeps your dryer working at greater efficiency. When not cleaned on a regular basis, the machine takes longer to dry your clothes, which wastes electricity.

444. Shake out your clothes before putting them in the dryer. This increases surface area, drying your clothes faster.

445. Wash your swimsuits properly. You can ruin a good swimsuit by washing it improperly. Rinse the swimsuit immediately after wearing. Then when you get home, soak it in cold water with mild hand soap for half an hour. To dry, lay the swimsuit flat on a towel, roll up the towel, and squeeze gently. Remove the swimsuit from the towel and lay on a flat surface to dry. Never wash your swimsuits in a washing machine or dry them in a tumble dryer. Never hang your swimsuits, as it stretches the fabric. Never dry your swimsuits under sunlight, as it fades the colors.

446. Do not over-dry your clothes. Over-drying wastes electricity. It also wears out your clothes faster, especially elastic. Those nice dress socks you over-dried will fall and expose your furry legs at the worst moments. Over-drying can also shrink cotton. Unless you want to cook your clothes and wear a melted dress shirt to your next business meeting, avoid over-drying.

447. Remove dry-cleaned clothes from their plastic bags. Clothes need to breathe. The plastic bag traps in moisture, causing yellowing or even mildew.

448. Dry clean at home. The average household spends $500.00 on dry cleaning services per year. Dry cleaning at home costs only a fraction of what you pay at the cleaners. Buy a box of Woolite Dry Cleaner's Secret for $19.99 on Amazon. The mega size has 14 loads, and each load cleans four garments, which means you can wash 56 garments.

Chapter 9

Transportation

Affordable Transportation

449. Use public transportation. Cars are fast and convenient, no doubt. However, driving is far more expensive than public transportation. In addition to paying for the car, you must pay for other expenses, such as insurance, gas, and maintenance.

450. Move close to public transportation. Living close to public transportation encourages you to use it more often.

451. Walk to your destination but not back. The MTA in New York City raises the fare every two years, but the service gets worse and worse. I would not mind paying an increased fare if the trains came on time because of it, but they don't. Now that rides are $2.75 each, which means roundtrip fares cost $5.50, I would rather walk if my destination is less than three miles away. I am willing to take public transportation on my way back though, so I save $2.75 each time. It does not sound like much, but it all adds up.

452. Live within walking distance from work. I lived within walking distance of almost every job I ever had. It was great because my commute was free, and I also knew exactly how long it took to get to work. Unless it was raining, a 15-minute commute was always 15 minutes. I was never scared of being late due to traffic or train delays.

453. Bike to work. Aside from the initial cost of the bike and the occasional maintenance cost, biking to work is free. It is also extremely healthy. Back when I attended community college, I biked five miles to school and then five miles back. It might seem like nothing, but it took me an hour to get to school every day because of all the traffic lights I had to obey. I didn't care though because I got great exercise, felt awake in class, and saved $116.50 by not paying MTA fares every month. At that point in my life, I was unemployed for several months and living off my savings, so every single dollar made a big difference.

454. Clean and maintain your bike regularly. Cheap bikes are not good, and good bikes are not cheap. Buy a good bike and then clean and maintain it regularly so that it lasts much longer.

Automobiles

455. Shop around. Email several dealers, even dealers that are out-of-state, requesting the price of the car you want. Sometimes an out-of-state dealer might offer a better price, including delivery, than your local dealer.

456. Buy the smallest car model that will fit your needs. Smaller cars are cheaper, get better gas mileage, and get cheaper insurance rates too. In Lubbock, several people drove pickup trucks even though they rarely used the cargo bed. I think they drive pickup trucks just because everyone else drives a pickup truck.

457. Keep your car longer. Before the Great Recession of 2008, people changed their cars every four to five years. Now that the economy isn't doing as well as before, people hold onto their cars for much longer. Hold onto your car for 10 years.

458. Buy a used not abused car with low mileage. A new car depreciates in value the moment you drive it off the lot. A new car loses 19 percent of its value in the first year of ownership.

Think about that for a moment. You buy a new car worth $20,000.00 and next year it is worth only $16,200.00. You might as well have bought a one-year-old car and thrown $73.07 in cash out of your window every single week.

459. Have one car per household. Sell your extra cars! When I was in Washington, D.C., I met a man at a museum who seemed very interested in learning personal finance from me. I told him that we would keep in contact. It turned out that he owned three cars, two of which were still on loan. I told him to sell his two cars and just keep one. Why would anyone who is single need more than one car? The extra cars require insurance, gas, and car payments. He said no. I can teach people how to save money, but if they are not willing to do the work, they will not get the results they want.

460. Be on the lookout. A friend of my friend Robert was driving through Albuquerque, NM. A gigantic ball of tumbleweed hit the side of his car and totally wrecked it. Unfortunately, the car was financed. Whenever he spoke about his car, he said, "I had a car, and I'm still paying for it!"

461. Buy the car instead of leasing. Buying a car is always cheaper than leasing in the long run.

Gas and Oil

462. Buy a fuel-efficient car. Aim for a car that can get almost 40 miles per gallon or possibly even more. One driver got 168 miles per gallon out of the 2006 Honda Insight by using hypermiling techniques. A fuel-efficient car will save you thousands of dollars over its lifetime.

463. Use regular gasoline. Unless your vehicle's manual specifically requires premium gasoline because it has a high-performance engine, use regular gasoline. Premium gas costs 20 cents more than regular gas.

464. Check gas prices on GasBuddy.com. On the website, type in your zip code. You should get a list of the lowest gas prices in your area. In my parents' area in Brooklyn, NY one gas station charges $2.65 per gallon, and another gas station charges $2.85 per gallon at the time of this writing. That is a difference of $0.20 per gallon! Right now, in Chelsea, MA where I live, gas is $2.44 per gallon. I work in Boston, MA though and the gas station down the street from my office is $2.79 per gallon—a difference of $0.35. In the area of Lubbock, TX where I used to live, the difference between the cheapest gas station and the most expensive one is only $0.06 per gallon. Still, savings is savings.

465. Pump your own gas. Self-service is cheaper than full-service.

466. Keep your car properly tuned. A poorly tuned engine uses up to 20 percent more gas.

467. Clean your car's air filter every month. A dirty air filter reduces gas mileage by as much as 10 percent.

468. Hypermile. Change the way you drive. Learn driving techniques that improve your car's fuel efficiency by as much as 37 percent.

469. Combine errands. Do all your errands back-to-back instead of making multiple trips. Even if you drive and save only 10 miles per week, you save 520 miles per year. If you take public transportation, the savings add up too. For instance, say I need to go to Manhattan from Brooklyn, and the fare is $2.75 per ride. I group all my errands in Manhattan into one day, so instead of making two separate trips with four rides ($11.00), I make only one trip with three rides ($8.25). Sometimes I manage to use only two rides ($5.50) by using free bus transfers or walking.

470. Carpool to work. Share the car with two other people and take turns driving. This saves money on gas and reduces the annual mileage on your car.

471. Do not warm up your car. In cold weather, warming up your car and letting it sit idle for a period of time is a waste of gas. It also harms the engine. Only cars that are 30 years old should need to be warmed up, and I doubt your car is that old.

472. Change the oil and oil filter according to the car's manual. You might not need to change the oil every 3,000 miles. Cars nowadays can last longer between oil changes.

Repairs and Tires

473. Be wary of service contracts and extended warranties offered by the dealer. They have limited coverage, despite what the salesperson says. Sometimes you are better off finding a repair shop that you will always go to instead of buying a service contract or extended warranty. I have a friend who purchased a new car from a dealership (first mistake). When she was filling out the paperwork, the salesperson convinced her to buy a warranty that included regular maintenance. It was only after she moved 40 minutes away that she discovered the warranty only covered maintenance at that specific dealership and didn't even cover oil changes. She tried to cancel (or transfer to a dealership near her) but they wouldn't let her. She was stuck paying an extra $26 a month for six years! That was an extra $1,872, and she still had to pay for her oil changes herself.

474. Tape a hand mirror to your car. Pelin Mathis on *Extreme Cheapskates* was too cheap to pay for a new left-side mirror, so she taped a pink hand mirror onto her car instead. Brilliant idea!

475. Rotate your tires every six months. Rotating your tires slows down their wear and prevents damage to the shock absorbers and suspension system, which are expensive to repair.

476. Keep your tires properly inflated. This improves your gas mileage and makes your tires last longer.

477. Use the proper tires for your vehicle. Using the wrong tires could hurt your gas mileage.

478. Check fluid levels regularly. A bottle of fluid costs only a few dollars, while replacing a worn or broken part due to low fluids costs hundreds of dollars.

Chapter 10

Health and Medical

Health and Wellness

479. Get your daily sunshine. Your body naturally produces Vitamin D when your skin is exposed to sunlight, so there is no point in buying Vitamin D supplements that are not as effective.

480. Stay out of the sun between 10 am and 4 pm. Lower your risk of skin cancer by preventing sunburns. Chemotherapy and radiation treatments are expensive.

481. Wear good shoes. Podiatric surgeons are seeing an increasing number of female patients due to bunions, foot deformities, and foot injuries. Too many women put looks before health. Please, wear shoes with good support—not heels and not flats either. Foot surgery is expensive and avoidable if you are willing to take care of your feet.

482. Always wear socks when outdoors. When my friends and I were spending our day at the leisure pool, I was extremely excited to jump into the water. I took off my sandals without realizing I stepped into a big swarm of ants. Two ants bit my tiny toe to avenge the death of their friends. I was lucky my toe only became swollen instead of getting a nasty infection. An allergic reaction to an ant bite, or any insect bite, could land you in the hospital and leave you owing thousands of dollars in hospital bills.

483. Wash your hands with soap. Sixty-two percent of men and 40 percent of women do not wash their hands after using the toilet. Your hands are covered with millions of bacteria. If you get sick, you must take off from work and pay for doctor bills and medications. By the way, to the men reading this, please wash your hands, especially after peeing. Just because your hand touches your penis without touching your urine doesn't mean your hand is clean! To not get into too much detail about this touchy subject, do your research on perianal sweat and the reason why you should wash your hands. We live in a first-world country where water and soap are freely available everywhere. Yet, people leave the bathroom without washing their hands.

484. Drink more water. Water is free! Most people do not drink enough of it.

485. Limit the amount of alcohol and soft drinks. Americans spend approximately 1 percent of their income on alcohol every year. That means that if you make $40,000.00 per year, you spend about $400.00 on alcoholic beverages every year. That money could go toward something else. As for soft drinks, soft drinks are loaded with sugar, and they boost the risk of stroke, obesity, kidney damage, certain cancers, high blood pressure, gum disease, heart attack, diabetes, and much more. I am sure you do not want to pay high medical bills anytime in the future.

486. Quit smoking. Cigarettes are expensive. If you smoke one pack of cigarettes per day right now, you save over $1,000.00 per year by quitting smoking. Smokers also pay higher health insurance premiums than nonsmokers.

487. Quit using drugs. Using drugs regularly could cost you thousands of dollars per year. People with drug addictions also tend to lose their jobs and damage their family relationships too. I understand that life is tough, and people use drugs to cope. However, using drugs is an extremely destructive habit.

488. Wear your helmet when biking. I have no idea why bicyclists do not wear helmets. Is it inconvenient? Is it uncomfortable? Seventy-five percent of fatal crashes involve a head injury. Ninety-seven percent of bicyclists who died in accidents were not wearing a helmet. If you do not wear a helmet and you survive an accident, you have the fortunate opportunity of paying hospital bills. Lucky you!

489. Lose weight. I had a student named Lori who had six-figure student loan debt from law school. She was one of my most motivated students. Everyone was so proud of Lori. Every time I taught a class, Lori brought her own homemade salad for dinner. Lori came directly from work, so she wanted to fill her stomach without paying too much money. Salads are great, as they are both cheap and healthy. How does losing weight relate to saving money? Lori lost weight naturally just by spending less on food. Losing weight also decreases your risk of heart problems, high blood pressure, diabetes, and certain types of cancer, which translates to having fewer medical bills.

490. Exercise. People who exercise regularly have lower medical costs.

491. Exercise at home. You do not need a gym membership to become fit. There are so many workout videos that you can follow along with on YouTube. My favorite YouTube channel is Fitness Blender. Kelli and Daniel from Fitness Blender make health and fitness attainable, affordable, and approachable for the average person. They also promote a healthy body image.

492. Attend donation-based yoga classes. Yoga classes in the United States are overpriced. There are several donation-based yoga classes out there, especially in urban areas. For example, in New York City, Yoga to the People is quite popular. All classes have a suggested donation of $10.00, but there is no lower or upper limit.

Doctors

493. Ask for itemized bills. You should know exactly what the doctor is charging you for. The itemized bill should contain a detailed breakdown of the costs for all services.

494. Review bills for errors. Compare the services and medications you received to what you were charged for. Sometimes there is an error.

495. Ask for an audit. Ask the healthcare provider and the insurance company to audit your medical bills. Sometimes the insurance company bills you incorrectly for the services and medications you receive.

496. Pay cash. Some physicians give discounts to patients who pay cash, as they avoid filing insurance claims and paying credit card transaction fees.

497. Say no to CareCredit. CareCredit is by far the worst kind of credit for medical care you can get. CareCredit capitalizes on people who need medical care by offering zero interest rates for a certain period. There is a catch, though. For instance, my husband needed to get a root canal procedure done, which cost $1,602.00. The dental office staff offered to let us finance the procedure using CareCredit. With CareCredit, we would get zero interest for the first year and then a 26.99 percent interest rate after one year. If we pay it off in less than one year, then great. If we do not, we would get charged 26.99 percent in interest, compounded daily from the first day we borrowed the money! That means that even if we owed only $5.00 after one year, we would be charged compounding interest going back to the first day, which would be $496.14 in interest. A $1,602.00 loan means $2,098.14 exactly one year from now. With such a high-interest rate, most people would be in debt forever. I adamantly refused to finance my husband's root canal procedure because of such crummy practices. The office staff heard this and said, "Good! Listen to Annie. She knows what she's talking about." Apparently, many people fall into the CareCredit trap and never get out.

498. Do your research. Some doctors charge more money just because they can. With the internet, you can look online to see whether you are getting a better-than-average, average, or worse-than-average price for a certain procedure.

499. Shop around. Ask for the estimated cost of a procedure or service before scheduling an appointment. You might find that the cost varies by hundreds of dollars at different clinics.

500. Visit an urgent care center instead of the emergency room. Urgent care centers are an affordable option for people who need immediate care but not emergency care. My friend Pessy had a fly in her ear and went to an urgent care center. The service was fast. However, be careful. The daughter of my friend Bob had a urinary tract infection and needed antibiotics. Bob is a very well-formed critical thinker. The urgent care center staff insisted on sending his daughter to the hospital for more testing. Bob said no and had to fight with them to get the antibiotics she needed. When he and his daughter got home, he researched the urgent care center and the hospital. It turned out that the urgent care center got a commission for every patient they sent to the hospital, so the staff might not be in your best interest!

501. Say no to more tests. Many doctors at hospitals tend to order high-cost diagnostic tests that are routine but completely unnecessary. When the mother of my friend Tippy had trouble breathing, Tippy took her to the hospital. The hospital ordered an X-ray, a CAT scan, and an MRI scan and stuck a tube up her mom's urethra because apparently, peeing into a cup was not sanitary enough. The mom ended up getting a urinary infection, which of course she had to pay money to get treated. The mother ended up staying in the hospital for several days, only to finally send her home with a blood thinner to prevent clotting. Question your own primary care physician too. Ask whether a test is necessary, especially if you have a high out-of-pocket deductible and copay.

502. Use in-network care providers. If you use an in-network provider, the insurance company pays for most of the cost. You just pay the copay. If you use an out-of-network provider, the insurance company pays for only part of the expenses, and you are responsible for the remaining amount.

503. Open a health savings account. These accounts allow people to pay for current and future healthcare expenses. The benefit of health savings accounts is that contributions are tax-deductible, and any interest earned is tax-free. Withdrawals are also tax-free so long as the money is used for qualified medical expenses.

Dentists

504. Have good teeth for life. I asked an endodontist whether this is possible, and he told me yes. He once had a 95-year-old patient who needed a root canal done. This patient went through her entire life, getting only dental cleanings twice per year and had no cavities. Nothing! At 95 years old, one of her teeth cracked, which led her to visit the endodontist. The endodontist did a procedure on her, and she never came back, so we assume she never had problems after that. My mom is another case. Right now, she is 58 years old and still has all her teeth. She gets a dental cleaning twice per year, and every time, the dentist takes only two minutes to finish. Her teeth and gums are completely healthy—not a single cavity. While genetics play a role in having good teeth for life, your daily habits play a bigger role. You can have good teeth for life if you are willing to take good care of them.

505. Brush your teeth for two minutes once in the morning and once at night. Some people skip brushing their teeth in the morning because they think brushing the previous night is sufficient. If you skip brushing in the morning to save toothpaste, you are flushing money down the toilet in the long term. Bacteria develop overnight while you are sleeping.

506. Brush your teeth properly using the bass brushing method. This might be surprising to hear: you have been brushing your teeth wrong all this time. As children, most of us learned to brush our teeth in circular motions. You might also think the harder you brush, the better. When you do this, you are scrubbing away the precious enamel and causing receding gums. The perfect way to do it is the bass brushing method, which is a scientifically proven method. You are supposed to lightly brush at a 45-degree angle along the gum line where most of the bacteria reside. Look on YouTube for a professional video demonstration.

507. Use a soft toothbrush with a small head. The softness prevents damage to your enamel. The small head makes it easier to brush every nook and cranny in your mouth. I like to use a toothbrush made for kids.

508. Skip the electric toothbrush. While a manual toothbrush costs between only $2.00 to $8.00, an electric toothbrush can go from $20.00 to $200.00. A higher price tag does not necessarily mean better performance. If you brush your teeth using a manual toothbrush and the proper technique, your teeth will be just as clean. However, if you are debilitated or physically impaired, do not follow my advice on this.

509. Use less toothpaste. Advertisements for toothpaste show a glob of toothpaste completely covering the toothbrush, which is done on purpose. The more toothpaste you use each time you brush, the more you buy. You can get your teeth just as clean by using a quarter of what the manufacturers recommend.

510. Floss your teeth once per day. This is something so basic, yet only 50 percent of all Americans floss daily. Brushing your teeth is not enough because it does not get rid of the plaque between your teeth. If you do not floss, you only clean 60 percent of your teeth's surfaces. Flossing will prevent gum disease and cavities.

511. Floss your teeth properly. There is no point to flossing if you are going to do it wrong. Learn the proper technique by watching YouTube videos by dentists.

512. Use an oral irrigator. I recommend using the Waterpik Cordless Freedom Water Flosser WF03. This is the cheapest model sold by Waterpik and costs only $39.95 on Amazon. It comes with no bells and whistles, but it gets the job done. Now, using the Waterpik is not a substitute for flossing. However, if you combine the Waterpik with flossing, your teeth will be extra clean.

513. Ditch the mouthwash. Save your $6.00. Mouthwash can freshen your breath temporarily, but it does not fix the source of your bad breath problem. Mouthwash also contains alcohol, which leads to a super dry mouth and more bacteria. This makes your breath smell even worse in the long term. Also, mouthwash is not an acceptable replacement for brushing and flossing single every day. Flossing and brushing, combined with regular dental cleanings, are enough to keep the mouth healthy. If you insist on including mouthwash in your daily regimen, use an alcohol-free one.

514. Rinse your mouth with water after every meal. Swish vigorously with plain water after you eat or drink something other than water. Repeat several times as required. I used to not do this in public until my husband taught me how to cup my hands together to scoop the water into my mouth. Now I do it all the time. As soon as I am finished eating, I head to the bathroom to do my ninja swishing.

515. Schedule regular cleanings. Go to the dentist twice per year to clean your teeth. The national average cost of a dental cleaning for someone without insurance is only $82.08. That is only $164.04 per year. Can you designate $13.67 in your budget every month toward your dental cleaning? This is an affordable price, and you save money in the long run. The dentist can spot problems immediately. Cavity fillings are much cheaper than root canals, crowns, and extractions. My dad used to work for the New York City MTA, and he had dental insurance through his employer. He refused to get dental cleanings for over a decade even though they were free! Today at 55 years old, he already has four root canals and a few of his teeth pulled. He has spent thousands of dollars on dental procedures because of his previous decisions. You do not want this to happen to you.

516. Quit whitening your teeth. Americans spend $1.5 billion annually on nonprescription teeth whitening products. Dentists report that bleaching is the most requested procedure among patients ages 40 to 60. Aggressive bleaching agents damage the enamel. The damage can be permanent if done repeatedly. With weakened teeth, you are more susceptible to gum disease later. You will pay thousands of dollars more in a few years to fix those problems. Teeth naturally darken with age, and yellow teeth are stronger than white teeth. There is no natural way to whiten your teeth. However, if you want your teeth to stop getting any darker than normal, then quit smoking cigarettes and drinking red wine and coffee.

517. Use free or low-cost dental providers. Many dentists provide services on a sliding scale to low-income patients who lack dental insurance. Do your research online to see which dentists in your neighborhood operate on a sliding scale.

518. Go to the dentist at your local dental school. You pay a reduced cost, and in exchange, dental students get to practice on your teeth. I only recommend this for basic procedures such as cleanings though.

519. Ask for a cash discount. By paying cash, you save the dentist from paying credit card fees and experiencing other billing hassles. Tell your dentist you will pay in full at the time of service in exchange for a cash discount.

520. Purchase a dental discount plan. My husband had no dental insurance so he purchased a discount dental plan from a general dentist. It costs only $75.00 per year, and all dental work in that office gets discounted by 30 percent.

521. Find a part-time job with dental benefits. Truthfully, I have never had a job that offered dental benefits. The only one that offered it was the Overton Hotel, and they only offered benefits for full-time employees. Some companies are more flexible. If you can find a part-time job with dental benefits, then get it.

522. Barter services. If your dentist runs a private practice, then you might be able to help the business gain exposure or run more efficiently by offering your services in exchange for dental work. You can offer accounting, marketing, designing websites and graphics, etc. I never tried this myself, but I served at a banquet once where a periodontist was the main speaker. He taught the attendees how to do a certain procedure and told them to charge thousands of dollars for it and to not feel guilty about doing it either. Why? Because they can get away with it when patients are in pain. He made a joke about not having to barter services anymore. Based on what I heard, I think dentists are willing to barter services sometimes.

523. Engage in dental tourism. Everyone knows dental work costs a ridiculous amount of money in the United States.

Many Americans cross the border into Mexico for dental work. To save money, see if the travel arrangements and dental procedure would be cheaper than doing it in the United States. Make sure you do your research on the foreign dentist beforehand. I have a story of my own. My husband needed a crown, and in Lubbock, TX where we lived, the lowest price he could get it for was $1,040.00. In New York City, he could get it for $500.00. (That low price is surprising—I know. I think it is because there are more dentists in New York City, so the pricing is more competitive. In Lubbock, your options are extremely limited.) A roundtrip plane ticket was around $400.00, and he stayed at my parent's place. So, for almost $1,000.00, he got not only a crown but also a short vacation in New York City.

524. See a good specialist for major dental procedures. When my husband needed a molar root canal, he saw a general dentist my father recommended. The general dentist charged only $500.00, but he missed a canal, which could lead to an abscessed tooth later. So, months later, my husband had to see an endodontist (specialist) for root canal retreatment before putting on a crown. That endodontist charged us $1,767.00 for the retreatment. That's right. We tried to save money in the beginning, but we ended up wasting money because the first dentist did a terrible job. When it comes to your teeth, don't skimp on seeing a good specialist. If you do, you might end up paying more in the future.

525. Straighten your crooked teeth. Crooked teeth are not just an aesthetic problem. Crooked, overcrowded teeth interfere with proper chewing and increase your chances of gum disease. Why? Removing food particles between crooked teeth is much harder than between straight teeth. Over time, incomplete plaque removal can lead to bleeding gums and gum disease. When teeth are misaligned, and you bite down, it causes a problem in the foundation of the teeth. Basically, you can lose your teeth. If you straighten your teeth with braces for around $4,900.00, you have a higher chance of keeping your teeth later in your life. Invisalign is a cheaper option for some people, but not everyone can use Invisalign as their treatment plan. In my case, I had an adult canine tooth that never came out, so the orthodontist had to expand my jaw over time, move my upper teeth to the left and right with braces to make enough space for a tooth, and then the canine tooth grew out from the gum. There is no way Invisalign could do that. For those of you who do not care about losing your teeth, think about how losing your teeth will affect your overall health. Missing teeth will make you change your diet and weaken your immune system.

526. Find an orthodontist who can straighten your teeth without extracting any teeth. When I was 12 years old, I wanted to get braces. The first orthodontist I saw told me I had to extract four teeth. Four perfectly healthy teeth! Was she out of her mind? My parents took me to several orthodontists before finding one who said he could straighten my teeth without any teeth extractions. This orthodontist did an excellent job on my teeth. I was so close to removing four healthy teeth, and I am glad I didn't. If anyone reading this is living in New York City, I recommend Hu Lin Orthodontics.

527. If you get braces, clean your teeth well. When I had braces, I constantly had swollen gums because it was difficult to floss and brush. You want to stay cavity-free while wearing braces. That way, you save money on dental cleanings and cavity fillings.

528. Wear your retainer after your braces are removed. My cousin had braces and then did not wear his retainer after he got them removed. His teeth moved back to the original position in less than a year. Thousands of dollars were wasted in this situation. For 12 months after your braces are removed, wear them continuously. After that, wear your retainers at night 35 times a week for the rest of your life.

529. Try jaw exercises and therapy first before considering surgery. For some reason, my jaw made a click or pop sound every time I opened my mouth. Sometimes it hurt so I couldn't sleep well. My face always felt tense from this. I thought this couldn't be fixed, but one day I came across jaw exercises for TMJ. I wasn't even sure if I had TMJ because I never went to the doctor to get diagnosed. I did the jaw exercises every night anyway, and within three days, my jaw stopped popping. I still do the exercises occasionally.

Optometrists

530. Get insurance-provided glasses. The frame selection is limited, and the designs are not the best, but the insurance covers for all of it. I bet that out of the designs they have, you can find a pair of frames that look suitable on your face.

531. Take advantage of promotions. When I needed new glasses but had no insurance, I saw that Stanton Optical was running a promotion for two eyeglasses and a free eye exam for only $69.00. Seeing that most places charged around $50.00 for an eye exam, the promotion was a steal. Again, the selection was limited, but I was still able to find frames that looked nice on my face.

532. Keep your old frames. You can get a new prescription while keeping your old frames that are still in good condition. When you do need to buy new frames, pick classic styles instead of trendy ones so you can always keep the frames for a few years.

533. Get your eyeglasses in Asia. My husband paid $20.00 USD in South Korea, and this included the eye exam, the frames, and the lens. He's been wearing the same eyeglasses for five years.

534. Get an eye exam at the optometrist and then fill your prescription at Walmart vision center, Costco optical, or even online. You will find better prices there than at your local optical shop.

535. Check your eyes less often. Check your eyes every other year instead of every year.

536. Skip most of the add-ons. The only add-on that is worth getting is the anti-reflective coating.

537. Order contact lenses online. Online websites usually give you the best price.

Medications

538. Dumpster dive for medications. A pregnant woman named Angel Durr on *Extreme Cheapskates* did this. She does not want to pay for anything, including medications and prenatal vitamins. Angel searches through pharmacy dumpsters for expired folate acid but says, "Don't try this at home."

539. Use antihistamines as a sleeping aid. The over-the-counter sleeping aids are basically repackaged antihistamines that are sold at higher prices. I didn't find this out until I got ant bites and my husband made me take an antihistamine. I took the pill and then headed off to pick up my work uniform and timecard. It was extremely embarrassing to falsely give the first impression as someone who is drowsy and would rather be elsewhere.

540. Buy the EpiPen overseas. The price of EpiPens in the United States increased by over 400 percent from 2008 to 2016. Why should you pay $600.00 for a twin pack of EpiPens when you can get the same exact thing for $100.00 in Canada and overseas? This outrageous pricing is the work of the greedy pharmaceutical company, Mylan. Update: I developed mild food allergies. While not life-threatening, my doctor recommended I keep an EpiPen around at all times because I have mild reactions now, but that doesn't mean I won't have severe reactions in the future. I'd rather spend the money than take my chances. My health insurance won't cover it. After some researching, I discovered CVS sells a twin pack of their low-cost epinephrine autoinjector, a generic alternative to the EpiPen, for a cash price of $109.99.

541. Buy generic brand prescriptions and over-the-counter drugs. The active ingredient in generic drugs is the same in name-brand drugs, and the effects are the same too.

542. Ask your doctor to write you a three-month prescription for medications you take on a regular basis. That way, you pay one copay fee instead of three.

543. Ask your doctor for an over-the-counter alternative. There might be a cheaper, effective over-the-counter drug that can treat your symptoms.

544. Combine pills. If you take several medications for the same condition, ask your doctor whether there is a single pill that can do everything.

545. Split pills. If it is cheaper to do so, ask your doctor to prescribe you half as many double-strength pills and then split them into two using a pill splitter.

546. Ask the pharmacy for the cost of the prescription with and without applying insurance. Someone with health insurance could be paying $900.00 for medications in addition to paying monthly premiums, and someone without insurance could be paying only $45.00. I know this sounds counterintuitive and wrong and unfair, but apparently, that is the way it is. It is difficult to explain why, because the health insurance industry in the United States is complicated. The next time you buy prescription medicine, try this.

547. Call multiple pharmacies. Before filling your prescription, call multiple pharmacies and ask for their prices. Neighborhood pharmacies might be able to give lower prices. If you must go to a chain, try Costco, which generally has the lowest price. Costco posts their drug price list online and you do not have to be a member to buy medication at the pharmacy.

548. Forget about gender differences when it comes to over-the-counter medications. For instance, Excedrin Menstrual Complete, Excedrin Extra Strength, and Excedrin Migraine are all the same products with the same active ingredients and the same dosage, just packaged differently. However, Excedrin Menstrual Complete, which is marketed toward women, is priced higher. This gender-based pricing is called "pink tax," where there is an upcharge in price for cosmetic differences (fragrance or color) in comparable products for men, that are directed toward women.

Nutritional Supplements

549. Buy nutritional supplements in bulk. Buy a three-month or six-month supply of supplements instead of 30 days' worth. Check the expiration date and calculate the amount you need to ensure you will finish your supply.

550. Combine supplements. Some supplements are sold with others because they contribute to keeping the same area of the body healthy. For example, calcium and magnesium are sold together because they both promote bone health.

551. Ask your doctor what supplements you need. Everyone's body is different. Some people need more calcium, while others need more iron. Vegetarians need vitamin B12 supplements while carnivores get vitamin B12 through their diet. Talk to your doctor to find out what supplements you need instead of buying multivitamins.

552. Stop buying nutritional supplements completely. There are no clear benefits from taking supplements (Haspel, 2020). Supplements do not prevent, treat, or cure chronic illness or disease. This has been scientifically proven. Some supplements even cause premature death (Molina, 2019). Get your vitamins and minerals the old-fashioned way by eating whole foods.

Chapter 11

Insurance

Homeowners Insurance

553. Improve your home security. Most insurance companies will give you a discount for installing a smoke detector, a burglar alarm, deadbolt locks, and a sprinkler system. Call your insurance provider to ask what safety features qualify for a discount before installing anything.

554. Purchase your homeowners insurance and auto insurance from the same company. They might give you a discount for buying multiple policies.

555. Avoid flood areas. Areas that are prone to flooding are extremely expensive to insure. Some insurance companies refuse to cover flood areas altogether.

556. Insure for the right amount. Insure for the cost of rebuilding your house, not the home's market value or the value of the land.

Renters Insurance

557. Get renters insurance. Tenants who get their personal property damaged or stolen are not covered by their landlord's homeowners insurance. In 2015, I moved into a house with eight other roommates. A few months later, the property manager suggested I move to another property under his management that was much nicer. I was hesitant at first, but I said yes to his offer. Three months after I moved out, the old house where I lived caught on fire. In fact, the fire started in my old room! I feel like I dodged a bullet. None of the tenants had renters insurance, and the fire destroyed all their personal property.

558. Decrease the policy limit on the renters insurance. The policy limit should be the amount that would cover the cost of replacing all your personal property. You should not get a higher policy limit than you need. To determine the value of your personal property, document it. Take a photo of everything you own and for each item, write the amount of money it should cost to replace the item as if you were to buy it brand new again.

559. Increase the deductible on the renters insurance. You lower your premium by raising the deductible, but you must be prepared to pay the deductible when you have to. Make sure you have a fully funded emergency fund before doing this.

Auto Insurance

560. Let your teenager start driving at 19 years old. After adding a 16-year-old teen driver to your insurance plan, expect to pay 95 percent more. If you wait until your teenager is 19 years old, your premium will only increase by 60 percent. You can also tell your teenager to pay for his or her own insurance. As a single policyholder, your teenager would end up paying only 18 percent more.

561. Get the "good student" discount on insurance for your teenager. If you still want to let your teenager drive at 16 years old, then brag about how he or she gets good grades. With the "good student discount," you pay from 6 to 20 percent less than the average rate.

562. Know when not to claim. For small accidents where no one was bodily harmed, consider whether you should skip reporting it. If you file the claim, you get money back, but the insurance company will increase your premium if it was your fault.

563. Raise the deductible on your auto collision insurance. Raise the deductible to $1,000.00. If you have an emergency fund of at least $1,000.00 in place, you have the money to cover the deductible in these situations.

564. Shop around for auto insurance. Get annual quotes from at least four insurance providers. If you have a good driving record, you might save money by switching to a different insurance provider.

565. Take a defensive driving course. Many people take defensive driving to drop a traffic violation. Another great reason to take a defensive driving course is that it can lower your insurance premiums. A six-hour online defensive driving course costs only $25.00.

566. Drive a car that is cheap to insure. Some car models require higher insurance premiums because they are more likely to be stolen, damaged, or repaired.

567. Drop collision and comprehensive coverage on old cars. If your car is more than five years old, fully paid off, and worth less than a couple thousand, it might not be worth it. Keep the liability coverage, though.

568. Say no to credit life or credit disability insurance. The car dealer will try to sell it to you when buying a new car. They are ridiculously overpriced, and the salesperson will try hard to persuade you to buy it so say no. Buy regular life insurance and disability insurance elsewhere.

569. Obey the speed limit. Avoid speeding tickets and increased insurance premiums.

570. Install a tracking device on your car. Many auto insurance companies have a tracking device that you can install on your car to monitor your driving habits. If you have good driving habits, you can get a discount.

571. Pay your auto insurance annually. More auto insurance companies are offering the option to pay monthly, but if you can pay annually, then do it. You can get a discount.

572. Get a low mileage discount. If you drive significantly less than the average number of miles per year, which is 13,474 miles, you can ask your auto insurance company for a discount.

573. Notify your insurance company about your car's safety features. If your car has automatic seat belts, airbags, and you also do not drink, tell your insurance company and ask for a discount.

Health Insurance

574. Get employer-based group health insurance if you have preexisting conditions or health problems. You get coverage with an affordable healthcare plan.

Disability Insurance

575. Have a longer waiting period. Opt for a three-month waiting period instead of a 30-day waiting period. This lowers your premium, but make sure you have enough emergency savings to support yourself for at least three months first.

576. Have a shorter benefit period. Choose to have the benefits payable until age 67 instead of for a lifetime. When you reach age 67, you are eligible for full Social Security benefits.

Long-Term Care

577. Buy long-term care insurance when you are 60 years old. Seventy percent of individuals over 65 years old need long-term care. Long-term care is very expensive. Buy the insurance while you still qualify and while the premiums are still low.

Life Insurance

578. Get life insurance only if someone else depends on your income. There is no point in getting life insurance if you are still single.

579. Buy term life insurance, not whole life insurance. The insurance agent will push you and try hard to convince you to buy whole life insurance, but do not buy it. It is much more expensive, meaning the insurance agent gets a bigger paycheck. Get term insurance for the length of time that you need. For instance, if your child is 10 years old right now, you only need to buy life insurance for the next 10 years.

580. Do not buy life insurance for your kids. Unless your kids contribute an income to your family, there is no need to insure their life.

581. Use an independent broker or agent. An independent broker or agent can show you quotes from many insurance companies. Also, stick with using the broker instead of going directly to the insurance company, as the quote you get will be the same.

582. Look for renewal guarantees when buying term life insurance. When your life insurance policy expires, you will be guaranteed renewal at the same price. If you do not get guaranteed renewal, then when your policy expires, you might have to pay a higher premium due to your age or deteriorating health.

583. Only buy as much life insurance as you need. Calculating the death benefit is not as simple as multiplying your annual salary by seven. If you let the salesperson do the calculations for you, you will most likely get a bigger death benefit than you need, and therefore a bigger premium. Do it yourself by estimating the amount that would meet your family's needs. Then subtract estimated Social Security survivor benefits and work-related policies. The remaining number is the amount that you need life insurance to cover.

Identity Theft

584. Try your best to prevent identity theft. If your identity gets stolen, you might end up owing a debt you never signed up for, get a fraudulent charge from another country on your card, or maybe even never receive your Social Security checks. Then you must waste time fighting with credit and banking institutions to fix the problems. While there is no guarantee that you can avoid identity theft for the rest of your life, there are precautions that you can take to ensure your identity remains safe.

585. Use a crosscut shredder. Crosscut shredders shred paper into small pieces as opposed to straight-line shredders that shred paper into strips that can be taped back together. In *That's So Raven* on Disney Channel, Raven's brother shredded the chemical formula for her school science project, and then Raven spent all night taping the paper back together. With a crosscut shredder that wouldn't have been possible.

586. Never click on popup advertisements. Clicking on them can install spyware onto your computer or can lead to your information getting phished.

587. Use strong computer passwords. Use a combination of lowercase letters, capital letters, numbers, and symbols, and make it more than 10 characters long. The best password is a random string of characters that you will never remember. Bitwarden is a free opensource password manager for individuals. You only have to remember the strong and long master password you've set for Bitwarden. I changed all my other passwords to be randomly generated. Even if you put a gun to my head asking me for the password to my bank account, I couldn't tell you! Also, none of my passwords are repeated. So, if I get hacked on one website, the incident stays isolated to only that website.

588. Avoid carrying too much identifying information around with you. You do not need to carry around your passport with you unless you are traveling internationally. If you are here in the United States as a visitor, then do carry your passport with you unless you have a driver's license or student ID. Never provide personal identifying information over the phone. Never leave personal documents lying around out in the open in your home. Likewise, never leave cash out in the open at home either because I can guarantee you that someone is going to take it, even your own spouse. My mom's friend's parents died years ago and in Chinese culture, people burn counterfeit money to honor deceased parents. One day the husband found $60,000.00 cash lying out in the open on the kitchen table. It looked real, but he assumed it was counterfeit, and then he took that money and burned all of it. His wife called, asking where the money went. She had taken the money out to make a big purchase. The husband realized he burned real money and started crying. His friends told him to cheer up because his parents passed away years ago. They didn't realize he was crying over the fact that he burned away his life savings.

589. Stop picking up phone numbers you do not know. Picking up can confirm to the person or robot on the other line that your phone number is still in service.

590. Secure incoming and outgoing mail. For incoming mail, use locked mailboxes and P.O. boxes. For outgoing mail, put your envelopes and packages in mailboxes instead of open mail trays.

591. Avoid giving out your social security number when possible. Sometimes it is unavoidable. Only give your social security number to the person in authority who wants it.

592. Regularly review credit reports. Check to see whether there are any suspicious charges or new credit cards that you did not open.

593. Only use cash at restaurants. If you give a credit or debit card to the server, the server swipes outside of your view. I do not mean to say that the server is a potential criminal. What I mean is that you do not know what happens between the time you give away your card and the time that you get it back.

594. Double-check information from phone calls. When my friend's sister went to Mexico, my friend got a phone call stating that her sister was being held hostage. The caller wanted my friend to send a few thousand dollars for ransom via Western Union. My friend was about to do it until she saw that her sister was active on Facebook Messenger. As it turned out, the sister was alive and well. The phone call was a scam.

595. Write your checks using uniball pens. Protect yourself from check-washing schemes. Uniball pens feature a special ink that cannot be washed away.

Chapter 12

Babies and Children

Babies

596. Decide to go childfree. This is a major life decision. It costs $245,340.00 to raise a child from birth to age 18. According to Pew Research, the number of American women choosing to go childfree has doubled since 1976. "Among all women ages 4044, the proportion that has never given birth, 18% in 2008, has grown by 80% since 1976, when it was 10%" (Livingston & Cohn, 2010). Many people claim that women who remain childless are selfish or career-minded. However, women can have children for selfish reasons too. For example, some women have children because they want someone to care for them in old age. If you want children, have good reasons and intentions.

597. Breastfeed your babies. In the first year of life, parents spend an average of $1,733.75 on baby formula. Breast milk is much cheaper than that! Breastfed babies also tend to get sick less often. See if you can get a breast pump from the hospital for free or if your insurance covers it.

598. Collect breast milk from other nursing mothers. When Apple Melecio on *Extreme Cheapskates* stopped producing breast milk, she collected breast milk from her friends. In her freezer, she had breast milk from five different women: Amy, Jessica, Brandi, Jennifer, and Megan. Apple's baby liked Jessica's breast milk the most.

599. Use homemade disposable baby wipes. You can make your own baby wipes using baby bath, baby oil, warm water, and paper towels (Blickenstaff, 2020).

600. Make reusable cloth wipes. Buy two yards of flannel fabric from JoAnn Fabric and Crafts using a coupon. Cut out 8" squares with rounded corners. You can get around 40 squares with two yards of fabric. Serge or zigzag the edges. Done.

601. Make your own cloth wipe solution. All you need is oil, soap, essential oils, and water. Look online for recipes. Make small batches. If you store the solution for too long, it comes musty and might even grow mildew.

602. Use reusable cloth diapers. The average baby uses 2,700 disposable diapers in the first year. At $0.20 per diaper, that is $540.00 per year. Buy between 30 and 36 diapers, which is enough for three days. Always wash cloth diapers within three days. Visit AllAboutClothDiapers.com for more information on cloth diapers.

603. Make cotton diapers instead of buying. Buy fabric and fasteners from JoAnn Fabric and Crafts, with a coupon of course. Find a free sewing pattern online and make it yourself.

604. Buy a convertible crib. Convertible cribs are more expensive than regular cribs but save money in the long run. When the baby grows older, you can convert the crib into a toddler bed.

605. Puree your own baby food. I worked in two grocery stores. You have no idea how many parents buy prepackaged baby food. Homemade baby food is cheaper, more nutritious, and less wasteful. Feed your babies the same food that you feed the rest of your family, but in puree form. Roast, steam, or boil vegetables or fruit and then puree in a mini food processor. Store in glass containers, place in the refrigerator and use in less than 48 hours.

Childcare

606. Ask your parents or grandparents to babysit. The average hourly babysitter rate for one child in the United States is $15.20. If you hire a babysitter every week, the costs add up quickly. I think this is a cultural phenomenon. In the United States, nuclear families are the norm, and newly married couples move away from their parents. In collectivist cultures, extended families are the norm, and new couples get a lot of help from relatives. Personally, my parents never hired a babysitter to take care of me. Instead, they sent me to live in China for the first three years of my life. My aunt and uncle took care of me while my parents paid for the costs associated with raising a child. The cost of living in China is much lower, so my parents saved both time and money. I came back to the United States when I was three years old and my parents still never hired a babysitter. They usually left me at home with my cousin Tony who was four years older than me. Later, my cousin Susan from China, who was already an adult, came to live with us, and she took care of me.

607. Take turns babysitting with a friend. If you have a friend with children, you can babysit their children. When you need babysitting, your friend can do it. Make sure you take turns, as you do not want your friendship to turn sour.

608. Form a babysitting coop. Parents in a babysitting coop take turns watching each other's kids. Parents gain points every time they babysit. As they gain more points, they can redeem those points when someone else watches your kids. If it works well, you get free childcare by offering free childcare for someone else.

609. Have a live-in sitter. Some adults do not make enough money to afford housing, or they cannot work at all due to disability. You can try offering a trusted adult a spare bedroom to live in for free. In exchange, that person cooks, cleans, and watches your children.

Clothing

610. Buy gender-neutral clothing. For clothing, buy gender-neutral for your first child. That way, when you have more children in the future, you can always reuse them. Don't force little Tommy to wear his older sister's pink dresses. I believe this tip applies to all parents, even for parents who do not plan on having more kids. After all, half of all pregnancies in the United States are unplanned.

611. Save clothing and hand it down. As a kid, I always wore my cousin's hand-me-downs. They made me look boyish and I hated it, which is why parents should try to buy gender-neutral clothing.

612. Buy one size larger for children's clothing and shoes. My parents did this when I was a child. When I was 12 years old, my mom bought clothes in the 14 to 16 age range. When my shoe size was size 6, my dad bought shoes in size 7. Children quickly outgrow sizes that fit just right. Let them wear bigger clothes so they can grow into them. That way, you do not have to shop for new children's clothes and shoes as often.

613. Buy the bigger-sized clothing and shoes when they are on sale and save them for future use. This way, you are always prepared. If you do not prepare, then the next time your kid complains about the pain from small shoes, you rush to buy new shoes when they are not on sale. You won't feel as sensitive to higher prices, as it is an urgent purchase. Some parents buy enough bigger-sized clothing and shoes to last for the next three years.

614. Accept freebies. When someone offers you free clothes, always say yes. You never know what might be in the bag.

615. Shop for secondhand children's clothing at yard sales or thrift shops. Kids love to play and make messes. The chances are high that your kids will either stain or ruin brand-new clothes. Secondhand clothes are cheaper. If they stain secondhand clothes, you won't feel as bad when it happens.

616. Ask for clothes for birthdays and Christmas. Ask family members to gift clothing instead of toys. Coats cost more than toys, so you save money that way.

617. Swap with other moms. Host a one-night children's clothing swap with any moms you know. Ask moms to bring bags of clothing they no longer need. From the pile that is there, they can take home the sizes that they do need.

618. Repurpose old clothes. For instance, use onesie extenders to add two to three months of additional wear to outgrown bodysuits. Cut off the feet of footed pajamas to turn them into pants when your kid grows too tall. Cut off the toes from outgrown socks to turn them into ankle warmers. Be creative with this.

619. Rent for special occasions. When it comes to adults, it makes sense to purchase formal clothes instead of renting. The clothes can be worn repeatedly. When it comes to children, however, renting makes more sense. Your kids might only wear the clothes once for a formal event. They might not wear them again because they might outgrow the clothes by the time another formal event comes around.

620. Cut your children's hair. Children's hair is very easy to cut and style. My mom cut my hair, my sister's hair, and my cousin's hair when we were all kids. I did not start going to the hairdresser until I was 14 years old. Also, when my cousin Tony moved to New Zealand and came back to visit for one month, he wanted my mom to cut his hair. He said he could never find a barber who cut hair like my mom did.

Toys

621. Collect abandoned toys at the playground. Apple Melecio on *Extreme Cheapskates* picked up a toy car at the playground for her daughter Chloe. It was missing two wheels, but she could still play with it.

622. Buy gently used toys. Young kids do not care whether a toy is new or used so long as they have something to play with. Check garage sales, Craigslist, eBay, and Goodwill.

623. Make your kids save up for their own toys. This teaches them to set goals and save for the things they want. Pay them an allowance based on the number of chores they do. They can save the allowance to buy any toy they want.

Chapter 13

Toiletries

624. Use all your partially used containers of personal care products. Before you ever buy a new bottle of shampoo, lotion, or anything else, finish what you already have.

625. Buy your personal care products in bulk size. Buying larger sizes reduces the unit price.

626. Buy one bottle for the entire household. If you have four people in your family, and everyone prefers using a different brand, you end up buying five different brands of everything. That means five bottles each of shampoo, conditioner, body wash, lotion, and face wash. This gets expensive and takes up too much space too. Make everyone agree on one brand or take turns picking the product.

627. Save hotel toiletries. Take them on your next trip, as sometimes hotels do not provide any. One hotel I stayed at in Mexico did not provide shampoo and conditioner. I was lucky I saved the toiletries from my previous hotel stay, so I dodged a midnight run to the local pharmacy.

628. Wash your face with only water. Children wash their face with only water, so why do adults have to use a facial cleanser? I suffered from acne since I was 10 years old, which led me to start using a facial cleanser. My acne got worse for the next 11 years. All that time, I tried a bunch of facial cleansers with salicylic acid and even gentle ones made specifically for sensitive skin. Nothing worked. My acne only cleared up after I started washing my face with only water. Not only did I save money, I also saved my skin.

629. Use kitty litter for facials. Pelin Mathis on *Extreme Cheapskates* saves money by using standard farm chemicals for her beauty products. Kitty litter with no added ingredients is basically bentonite clay, which is the main ingredient found in expensive facial masks.

630. Keep bar soap inside a soap dish far away from the showerhead. Drain out any water from the soap dish after you finish showering. Keep the bar soap as dry as possible, so that it lasts longer.

631. Keep small pieces of bar soap. Wet the small piece and then stick it onto a new bar of soap.

632. Use a dime-sized amount of shampoo and conditioner. Most people use too much. A dime-sized amount is enough to get your hair clean. Add more water to get a good lather. One 16 oz. bottle can last a whole year for a single person.

633. Use hair conditioner as shaving cream. The conditioner makes the hair softer, which makes it easier to shave.

634. Buy men's shaving cream and razors. Due to clever marketing, women pay more money for the same exact products that men use. The main noticeable difference is the color and the fragrance, but the formula is still the same. This is just another example of the pink tax mentioned in tip #549.

635. Use less lotion. Most people use too much lotion. If you rub an area more than twice, and the skin feels greasy, then you have used too much. Use enough lotion so that the skin absorbs the lotion in only two rubs.

636. Apply perfume only in certain areas. Only apply perfume behind your ear, at the bottom of your throat, on your wrist, inside your elbow, and behind your knee. Your perfume will last all day because the blood circulation produces heat. Some people apply too much perfume. Not only is it wasteful, but it can also give people around them migraines or allergic reactions.

637. Use reusable cotton rounds. You can use these to remove makeup or apply facial toner. To be honest, reusable cotton rounds are overpriced because they are marketed as organic, natural, and eco-friendly products. Make your own instead.

638. Use the huge cotton balls that come in pill bottles. They have been sanitized with hydrogen peroxide, so they are clean. You should remove the cotton balls from the pill bottles anyway, as they reduce the medicine's potency by pulling moisture into the bottle (U.S. National Library of Medicine, 2020).

639. Use a tube wringer to squeeze out every drop of toothpaste. Don't you get annoyed when you know there is still toothpaste left inside the tube, but nothing comes out? You flatten, you roll, you pinch, but it does not work. Use a tube wringer. I got one five years ago and never looked back.

640. Use reusable menstrual pads. I thought they were disgusting before I started using them. After all, nothing could be as sanitary as the pristine, white menstrual pads you buy in stores. As it turns out, disposable menstrual pads and tampons are carcinogenic and can even cause toxic shock syndrome. One model had to amputate her leg. Try using reusable menstrual pads. If you wash them properly, they never stain. Plus, since they are made from fabric, they feel the same as underwear when you use them. I found the best prices on Etsy.

641. Use a menstrual cup. Menstrual cups are the reusable substitute for disposable tampons. The most popular menstrual cup is the DivaCup. The DivaCup can be worn for 12 hours without leaks. They are also easy to clean.

642. Use handkerchiefs instead of facial tissue to blow your nose. It is not disgusting. Think of underwear—do you wear disposable underwear just because it gets dirty down there? No, you wash it. The same principle applies to handkerchiefs. There is an efficient way of folding a hanky for blowing your nose. You can get over eight folds without getting mucus everywhere in your pocket. At the end of the day, throw it in the laundry and grab a fresh one.

643. Quit wearing deodorants and antiperspirants. I have never worn deodorants or antiperspirants in my life. I believe that if you shower every day, you will not stink. Or it is possible I hit the genetic jackpot for not having stinky armpits. Just kidding—antiperspirants increase the number of odorous bacteria in your armpit, which means they make your body odor worse. When you stop wearing them, you get rebound odor. However, after a year, you stop stinking. Also, deodorants and antiperspirants contain neurotoxins and carcinogens. That alone should make you quit.

644. Be lucky enough to be born male. Men use less toilet paper because they do not wipe after they pee. This might also be why they are so quick in the bathroom.

645. Separate your two-ply toilet paper. For the amount of time you invest in doing this, you save about $10.00 a year. Personally, I would not do this, but it will save toilet paper.

646. Stop using toilet paper. Kate Hashimoto on *Extreme Cheapskates* said she does not believe in spending money on something that she is just going to throw away. Instead, she uses water, soap, and her hand to clean herself after using the toilet. Kate hates literally flushing money down the toilet.

647. Use a bidet. In an interview, a coloproctology specialist named Dr. Alexander Herold said, "water is just as important in toilet hygiene as it is for body hygiene. In the past, people even made sacrifices in their general body hygiene in order to save water. Nowadays, we shower almost daily, and this idea is practically inconceivable. When it comes to toilet hygiene, however, we are lagging behind. Pure water, either warm or cold, is always the most thorough and gentle cleaning method." Install a bidet on your toilet, and you will never have to buy toilet paper again.

Chapter 14

Cosmetics and Hair Care

Cosmetics

648. Paint your own nails. My mom's first business was a nail salon. Do you wonder how she got started? Never having painted nails before, she started working at a nail salon. After two weeks, she was sick of working there. So she started her own nail salon business, gave free manicures to the first two customers, and then started charging. Seriously, painting nails is so easy you can learn to do it yourself. If you can only paint with your dominant hand at first, then ask your significant other or housemates to do it.

649. Stop wearing makeup. American women spend $200,000.00 on average on cosmetics in their lifetime. Many women cannot leave their house without makeup on. One time, I attended a conference and had to share my hotel room with another college student named Christine. Christine took an hour to get ready in the morning because she had to apply makeup on her face. She kept pestering me to hurry up and get out of bed. I got up 45 minutes later than she did and still went to breakfast first because I do not wear makeup. I suffered from acne for 11 years, and still, I never wore makeup to cover it up. I learned to feel comfortable in my own skin. I only wear makeup when I really need to, such as for special occasions like job interviews or weddings, or for my YouTube videos, because what goes on the internet stays on the internet forever.

650. Use drugstore makeup brands. Drugstore makeup is cheaper than expensive department-store brands. There are many "Full Face Drugstore vs. High-End Makeup" videos on YouTube. The comparison looks very similar.

651. Use Johnson's No More Tears Baby Shampoo as a makeup remover. It is a cheap substitute and works just as well as normal makeup removers. Pour a dime-sized amount of baby shampoo on your hand and add a little water. Then lather it onto your eyes and skin and wipe the makeup off with a cotton round or the reusable rounds from tip #637.

652. Look on the top and bottom shelves. The most expensive makeup products are placed at eye level.

653. Reuse old mascara brushes from more expensive brands. Rinse the brush in hot water to remove clumps. Oftentimes, the brush is what makes the mascara expensive. The brush can be reused with cheaper mascara.

654. Pour the last drops of perfume into a bottle of unscented lotion. Perfume can be expensive.

655. Ask for sample sizes before buying a whole bottle of perfume. Try before you buy. Otherwise, you waste money on a product you do not like.

656. Use paintbrushes instead of makeup brushes. Why does MAC charge $35.00 for a single brush? No seriously, one time, I bought $200.00 worth of makeup products from MAC, and I wanted to buy some brushes too. The cheapest brush I wanted was $35.00. That is so overpriced. I bet they paid less than $1.00 in labor costs to manufacture it in China. Instead, I headed over to Sephora and bought a set of five brushes for $21.11. An even cheaper alternative is to use paintbrushes. They cost around $3.00 each at the local craft store.

657. Cut open bottles that are almost empty. You might get the last bits of moisturizer, primer, foundation, or concealer that you would be missing otherwise.

658. Buy a slightly darker shade of foundation or bronzer. Mix the foundation or bronzer with a little moisturizer to extend its use.

659. Recycle old Mac, Kiehl's, and Lush containers. You can get free products for recycling a certain number of containers.

660. Use custom magnetic palettes. You can save $3.00 by buying the refills instead of the standard product. In addition, some women realize they have multiples of the same color after depotting their collection. They save money by only buying colors they know they do not have. There are many instructional videos for depotting palettes on YouTube.

661. Revive your dried mascara instead of buying a new bottle. Do not add any water to dried mascara. It only dries it out even further. Instead, tighten the cap as tight as possible and then place the tube of mascara in hot water for two minutes. The dried mascara should be melted.

662. Spin your mascara wand instead of pumping. Pumping the wand traps air inside and dries out the mascara.

663. Protect your makeup compacts from breaking in your bag. Place a cotton ball or cotton round inside. Preventing your compacts from falling apart in the first place is less hassle than putting it back together.

664. Add a little rubbing alcohol to broken eye shadows and pressed powders. Crush the eye shadow or pressed powder into loose powder. Spray rubbing alcohol onto the eye shadow or pressed powder. Compress it with the back of a spoon and then let it dry. After it dries, clean the edges using a Q-tip and rubbing alcohol.

Hair Care

665. Cut your own hair using CreaClip. I have used Crea-Clip to cut my hair and my mom's hair for several years. CreaClip is a haircutting guide that helps you cut your own and other people's hair. All you need to do is clip it to your hair, slide it down, and cut along the guide. CreaClip is easier to use on straight hair but it can be used to cut layers for curly hair too. You just have to cut your hair when wet and add four inches to your desired length. It is generally a product made for women, but some men use it too. The original CreaClip costs $29.99. Knockoff versions are even cheaper.

666. Shave your head bald. I never knew shaving your head bald saved money until I met my husband. My husband's hairline started receding in his 20s, so he shaved his head completely bald. How does he save money? He shaves it himself (or he asks me to help him shave it) instead of going to the barbershop, so he never pays for haircuts. He uses body wash to clean his scalp instead of shampoo. The only product you will find in his bathtub is body wash—no shampoo, no conditioner.

667. Get free or deeply discounted haircuts at a local beauty school. Cosmetology students need people to practice on.

668. Get a cheap haircut. When I lived in Brooklyn, I paid $12.00 for a haircut at my local hair salon. I thought my hairdresser always did an excellent job and paid her $8.00 in tip every time I went, so I paid $20.00 for a haircut. Still, $20.00 for a haircut is cheap. The average American woman spends $44.00 on haircuts, plus $9.00 for tips.

669. Wash your hair at home before going to the hair salon. Some hair salons charge you less if you only go in for a haircut. If that is the case, then wash and dry your hair at home first before going. A wash, dry, and haircut will be more expensive than a haircut only.

670. Be content with your natural hair. Women with straight hair want curly hair. Women with curly hair wish they had straight hair. I find the same when it comes to color. Women with blonde hair want brunette and vice versa. Women pay hundreds of dollars per year for perms and color changes. All these chemicals dry out your hair and cause split ends, no matter how much you condition. Be happy with the hair you were born with. You have no idea how many people are envious of your hair. They just never tell you.

671. Dye your own hair. If you still want to dye your hair, then dye it yourself at home. With the rise of beauty channels on YouTube, there are plenty of instructional videos you can watch on how to dye hair at home. Most hair dyes cost less than $10.00, and lighteners cost less than $20.00.

672. Avoid washing your hair too often. Washing too often strips your hair of its natural oils. It also makes you go through the bottle of shampoo faster. Try washing only once a week. With time, your hair learns to regulate itself and produce less oil. If it gets too oily, use a boar's bristle brush to evenly distribute the hair's natural oil from the scalp to the ends.

673. Airdry your hair. I think my husband is so lucky to be bald because his head dries in five seconds with a towel. The rest of us are not as lucky. Airdrying your hair saves money on electric bills. If you want, you can airdry halfway by wrapping your hair in a towel for half an hour to absorb the water. Then finish off with the hair dryer.

674. Sew your own towel turban. Adding on to the previous tip, you can make your own towel turban instead of buying one at

Sally's Beauty Supply for $14.95. All you need is an old towel, a sewing machine, a spool of thread, an elastic band, a pair of scissors, and a sewing pattern. The sewing pattern is very simple, and you can find it online. Making my own cost only $2.00 since I already had some supplies at home. All I needed to buy was an elastic band.

Chapter 15

Cleaning Supplies

675. Reuse your towel. Dad, this one is for you! Quit tossing your used towel in the hamper every day. The house is not a hotel. If you take a shower and wipe your body dry with a towel, the towel is not that dirty. One towel per week per person is enough, two towels maximum.

676. Only use white sheets, towels, and washcloths. Colored towels fade over time and look dingy. White towels look better longer because you can bleach them. Bleaching too often will deteriorate fabrics though. Watch out!

677. Make your own cleaning products. Most homemade cleaning products use the same ingredients: baking soda, borax, castile soap, cornstarch, essential oils, lemon juice, salt, toothpaste, vinegar, and hydrogen peroxide. These ingredients are very cheap. Search on the internet for recipes. DO NOT mix cleaners together, as the fumes can be very dangerous.

678. Clean less often. If you clean less often, then you use fewer cleaning products.

679. Buy paper towels and toilet paper in bulk. The price per roll is significantly lower when you buy in bulk. This is hard to do when you're single because your income is most likely limited and it will take an eternity to finish the whole package. If you live with other people, buy in bulk and split the cost.

680. Buy paper towels and toilet paper based on unit price per square foot. Getting the best price for paper towels and toilet paper can be confusing. Each brand has different sizes, number of sheets per roll, and number of rolls per package. All brands use the words "big," "huge," "giant," "mega," and "super mega" on their packaging to make you think you are getting a great deal. To make it even more confusing, some paper towels are "double rolls." Some rolls of toilet paper are single-ply and some are double-ply. Use this handy-dandy formula to determine the cheapest price per square foot:

Price Per Square Foot = Total Price of the Package ÷ Total Square Feet of Paper in the Package

681. Use dishrags to clean countertops. This reduces the use of paper towels.

682. Use a foaming soap dispenser for hand and dish soap. Foamy soap is basically watered-down soap injected with air. It works just as well as liquid soap while using less soap. Buy a sturdy foaming soap dispenser. Fill the empty bottle with a ratio of 1:5 liquid soap to water and then screw the top on. Shake the bottle. Now it is ready for use. Refill when you run out.

Chapter 16

Education and Tuition

683. Send your children to public school. Stop paying an arm and a leg for private schools that are not inherently better than public schools. Parents, release the guilt you feel about sending your kids to public school.

684. Skip the test prep courses. In New York City, 8th and 9th-grade students take the Specialized High School Admissions Test. The exam score is the sole determinant of whether a student gets accepted into a specialized high school. Growing up, most of my friends were forced by their parents to take test prep courses for the exam, which cost thousands of dollars. Some had private tutors. My parents refused to pay for test prep; they bought two study books for $16.50 and told me to study on my own. I scored the lowest out of all my friends, but we all got accepted into Brooklyn Technical High School. Once I started high school, I had the highest grades out of all my friends and graduated in the top 5 percent of my class. I truly believe that test prep courses and private tutoring for the SHSAT, the SAT, the ACT, the GRE, etc. are a waste of money. Test prep courses increase your score by showing you tips and tricks and telling you what you should and should not focus on studying. They give you the shortcuts. They help get your foot in the door, but it does not mean you will do well once you get in. Think of it like this—if you have the self-discipline to sit down and study, you will do well. If you have the self-discipline to do anything you want to do in life, you will succeed. In life, there are no shortcuts.

685. Skip the national standardized tests. You can expect to pay around $350.00 for SAT and ACT registration and score report fees. I do not even include the cost of study materials and books. It is possible to get into college without ever taking the SAT or ACT—I'm a living example. I got into Kingsborough Community College then I transferred to Thomas Edison State University. FairTest.org has a list of accredited colleges and universities that do not need SAT or ACT scores to determine admission.

686. Skip going to college altogether. Only 52 percent of college students graduate. Those who drop out still must pay their student loans. Also, the job market looks bleak for recent college graduates: half are either unemployed or underemployed, which means they work jobs that do not require a college degree.

687. Learn on your own. Education does not have to happen inside an institution. You can self-study by reading books, watching videos and documentaries, and taking online courses. If you cannot learn on your own, take a class at your local community college for no credit. You get the education without the credentials.

688. Delay college. In European countries, high school seniors are encouraged to take a gap year and explore their interests before enrolling in college. I believe American parents should encourage their children to take a gap year. Seeing as at least half of all college students change their major at least once, taking a gap year is not such a bad idea. Public four-year universities and colleges charge $324.70 per credit on average. Most college courses are worth three credits each. Taking a few college courses that end up not counting toward your degree because you change your major wastes thousands of dollars.

689. Attend community college first and then transfer to a four-year college. Community colleges offer the lowest cost-per-credit, averaging $135.09 per credit. The class sizes are smaller, and the professors are not as focused on research, so they take the time to teach you. In addition, since half of all college students drop out, it is better to go to community college first. When you complete 60 credits at a community college, you get an associate degree. When you complete 60 credits at a senior college and drop out, you have nothing to show for it. For some reason, though, people look down on community college students as if they are somehow intellectually inferior. When I took a two-year break between high school and college, my relatives thought I must have been too stupid to go to college. That's Chinese culture for you. When I finally attended Kingsborough Community College, they said, "At least she got into the lowest-ranked school in New York City." I felt insulted that they never looked beyond the name of my school to get to know me more. Relatives like them aren't worth associating with anyway, though. By the way, I finished in three semesters instead of four, and I also graduated as salutatorian from Kingsborough Community College.

690. Attend an in-state public college. Enrolling in an out-of-state public university will cost you at least $10,000.00 more per year. In addition to paying the out-of-state tuition rate, you also pay for dormitory fees, meal plans, flights, and long car rides home. Attend an in-state public college to save money. If possible, attend one close to home so you can live with your parents while going to college. There is no shame in doing that. You have the rest of your life to live independently, after you graduate.

691. Stop caring about where you go to college. Forget about prestige. It does not matter where you go to college. Let me say it again: it does not matter where you go to college. Economists Alan Krueger and Stacy Berg Dale did a study on this in 1999. They compared the earnings of people who graduated from elite colleges to people who were admitted to elite colleges but chose to attend moderately selective colleges instead. Twenty years after graduation, both groups earned the same. The fact that you finish your degree matters much more than your alma mater. Did you ever ask your accountant where she got her degree? Did you ever care to ask your doctor where he went to medical school? I don't think so. Employers do not care either—only a small handful care. Skills and experience matter more.

692. Finish college earlier. If you can finish your bachelor's degree in three years instead of four, then go for it. To do this, you need to take 20 credits per semester. It is doable if you take 15 credits in the fall or spring, and then take an extra class or two in the summer and winter. I finished my associate degree in three semesters instead of four, which means I saved $2,600.00 by not taking the fourth semester. The average tuition rate at a four-year, in-state public college is $9,650.00. Thus, by finishing a year early, you save close to $10,000.00, and you can also start your career and make money earlier.

693. Take college-level courses in high school. College Board AP courses are available at most high schools. Also, some juniors or seniors in high school can enroll in College Now. Take advantage of AP courses and College Now programs while you are still in high school, as the cost-per-credit is low. By the time you graduate high school, you will have enough credits to enter college as a sophomore or junior. Some people enter college as juniors and finish their bachelor's degree in two years, saving around $20,000.00 if they attended an instate public college.

694. Test out of college. I tested out of a few college courses by self-studying and then taking CLEP and DSST exams. If you pass the recommended ACE score for CLEP and DSST, you get college credit. Each exam costs only $80.00, and the testing center fee costs between $25.00 and $40.00 per exam. Shop around to find the cheapest testing center. For instance, the first time I took a CLEP exam, I paid $38.50 at Brooklyn College. Brooklyn College also only proctored CLEP and DSST exams once a month, which meant I had to wait. I looked around and found Cambridge Business Institute, which offers exam proctoring five days a week and only charges $25.00 per exam. I took seven exams, received 21 college credits toward my bachelor's degree, and paid only $735.00. I saved around $6,069.00 by taking CLEP and DSST exams instead of taking classes. For more information on testing out of college, please visit DegreeForum.Wikia.com.

695. Take StraighterLine courses. On StraighterLine.com, you pay a $99.00 monthly subscription and approximately $59.00 per class. This is a cheap option if you can finish a bunch of classes in a short amount of time. I completed eight StraighterLine courses in three months. That means I paid $297.00 for monthly subscriptions and $472.00 for classes. For only $769.00, I received 24 college credits toward my bachelor's degree. I saved around $7,023.00 by taking StraighterLine courses instead of regular college courses.

696. Contribute to a 529 plan for your child. A 529 plan is a tax-advantaged savings plan for future college expenses. Contributions are not tax deductible, but earnings grow tax-free so long as the withdrawn funds are used to pay for qualified expenses. If your child graduates from college and the 529 plan still has money remaining, the plan can be rolled over to another beneficiary.

697. Look for programs in your college that offer financial support. The programs available vary from college to college. In the City University of New York, there are several programs available, such as SEEK, College Discovery, and ASAP. These programs provide money for textbooks and MetroCards. The only drawback is that these programs have eligibility restrictions. For instance, I joined the College Discovery program when I first entered Kingsborough Community College. I was lucky I passed by their booth during New Student Orientation, as the program is only available for new students. Had I found out about the program in my second semester, I would not have been eligible.

698. Take free college classes as a senior citizen. If you are older than 60 years old, see if your local college offers a tuition-free program. I know that Kingsborough Community College offers a program called My Turn. The program lets New York State residents over 60 years old attend college tuition free. I had many classmates who were My Turn students, and they always added a fresh perspective due to their life experiences.

699. Join the United States armed forces. The Military Tuition Assistance program pays up to 100 percent of tuition expenses if semester hours cost $250.00 or less. The Post-9/11 GI Bill covers the entire in-state tuition for state schools. I know veterans who did not have to pay a dime for their college education.

700. Apply for college scholarships during the summer. Apply to 4,000 scholarships—any scholarship you can find and are eligible for. One high school student spent an entire summer applying for college scholarships. She got rejected from most of them, but she got enough scholarships to pay for her entire bachelor's degree.

701. Borrow textbooks from the library. I always borrowed textbooks from the school library. The drawback was that I could only loan textbooks for four hours, and they had to remain in the library. Since this was inconvenient, I scanned entire textbooks with my iPhone using an app called Tiny Scanner. That way, I could always read the eBooks at home.

702. Rent your textbooks. It is cheaper than buying.

703. Buy older editions of textbooks. If you must buy textbooks, buy the used version of an older edition on Amazon. Publishing companies constantly release new editions for textbooks, even when the content is barely changed. The main thing that is different in newer editions is the page numbers, the homework questions, and a few pictures. They do this because they cannot make money from used-book sales, so they make the older editions obsolete by releasing new ones.

704. Pirate digital textbooks. Pirating movies, television series, and music involves major ethical concerns. Pirating textbooks, however, are another story. First, students are required to get the textbook. It is not optional. I once had a microeconomics professor who required a special edition of the textbook that could only be purchased at the school bookstore. It cost over $100.00 because the school bookstore had a monopoly on that book. Second, a textbook can cost up to $200.00, which is outrageous. Textbook prices have increased by 1,041 percent since 1977. Honestly, no student wants to pay $200.00 for a new textbook, end up never even opening it, and then trying to sell it after the semester is over for next to nothing.

705. Compare the cost of living on campus vs. off campus. The costs vary depending on which university you attend and how many people you live with. At some universities, a specific real estate group owns all the houses and apartments near the college. This monopoly on real estate causes rent to be artificially high. See if you can rent further away from campus to get a better deal. It takes longer to commute to campus, but it saves money. Also, if you live off campus, see if you can live with several roommates (e.g., four people in a two-bedroom apartment) to lower your share of the rent.

706. Borrow Federal Perkins Loans or Direct Subsidized Loans if you must finance your college education. I do not recommend taking out student loans to pay for college. However, if you must, then try to borrow Perkins Loans or Direct Subsidized Loans. At least your interest does not accrue while you are still in school.

Chapter 17

Books

707. Borrow books from the library. Growing up, I always borrowed books from the library. The deadlines motivated me to finish reading the book. I almost never buy books because I usually only read them once and leave them on a shelf to collect dust. Plus, borrowing books is a great way to test-run books. If you do not like the book, then return it. If you do like it, then buy it. Libraries are going more and more digital. Check to see if your library lets you rent eBooks through Hoopla or Libby and read them on your phone or Kindle.

708. Buy books in great condition instead of new. Unless the book is a gift, I always buy my books used. I can buy five or six used books for the price of one new book. If the content is readable and no pages are missing, what's the difference? New books eventually get old and dirty anyway, so might as well buy them used to start with. ABEBooks is a great website for you to check out.

709. Read free eBooks on Gutenberg.org. Project Gutenberg has 54,629 eBooks available for download. Most of the books are in the public domain.

710. Trade books on PaperbackSwap.com. List the books you want to swap with other members. When a member requests your book, mail the book via USPS Media Mail and pay for postage. In return, you get to request books, and you receive them with the postage already paid.

Chapter 18

Office Supplies

711. Reuse shipping boxes and envelopes. For shipping boxes, keep the ones that are still rigid. Remove any labels and cut the tape so that the boxes can be stored flat. For polyethylene envelopes, cut them with scissors whenever you receive any. Then flip them inside out so that the shipping label is no longer visible on the outside. When you need to mail small objects, use those and shut them with packing tape.

712. Use the free envelopes that come with bills and junk mail. Cover the envelope with a label and put your own stamp.

713. Use free shipping boxes from USPS. USPS offers free Priority Mail® boxes. You can order on the official website to get it delivered, or you can pick up at your local post office.

714. Print your own shipping labels. You can use PayPal to print shipping labels for small packages. Compared to going to the post office, you save money on first-class packages, and there is no waiting in line. You also avoid paying the $15.99 monthly fee that Stamps.com charges. You must have a PayPal account, a printer, paper, and a digital scale. This is the shortened secret link: https://goo.gl/pwFCx5

715. Use bubble wrap and newspapers for cushion when shipping packages. Packing supplies, such as Styrofoam peanuts, are expensive.

716. Reuse old calendars. Calendars can be reused because the days of the week repeat every few years. If you have a calendar you never opened, you can reuse it. WhenCanIReuseThisCalendar.com can tell you when your calendar can be reused.

717. Take free pens and pencils at business conferences. Keep doing this, and soon you'll have enough pens and pencils to last you a whole year.

718. Shop for school supplies during the back-to-school season. Staples has a Less List for School, which you can find at Staples.com/LessList. There, you'll find the lowest prices. In addition, Staples has a sale called Weekly School Steals. When I was a kid, my friends shopped for school supplies at Staples throughout the summer. They only bought what was on sale for that week. I am sure their parents saved a lot of money. My parents did not save much money on school supplies because they were always working. They did not have time to take me school supply shopping every week, so they only took me once before school started. Every year, I spent close to $130.00 on back-to-school supplies.

719. Know what school supplies you already own at home. Check your closets. Check everywhere! When my ex-boyfriend Jared was in college, he always bought new school supplies, as he lost track of what he already owned. His house was extremely cluttered. One day, I helped him declutter and put all his school supplies in a cabinet. He had enough looseleaf paper and spiral notebooks to last another two years.

720. Buy school supplies at the dollar store. I grew up in an Asian neighborhood in Brooklyn, NY. Dollar stores were everywhere. School supplies at the dollar store were usually half the price of merchandise at Rite Aid, CVS, and Staples. Examine the quality before buying, though. For instance, to save money, my dad always bought composition notebooks at the dollar store. The pages were thin. Every time I erased my writing, I ended up tearing the page and ruining my notes. By the way, I wouldn't skimp on pencils or erasers. Pencils that keep breaking or erasers that leave streaks and marks are not worth it!

721. Buy school supplies on sales tax holidays. Every state has its own sales tax holiday for designated products. In Texas, most school supplies (must be under $100.00 per item) are exempt from sales tax for one weekend in August. Visit SalesTax-Institute.com to find out when your state's sales tax holiday is.

Chapter 19

Subscriptions

722. Unsubscribe from magazines. Magazines have pretty pictures but tend to be devoid of any well-written information. Ninety percent of the magazine content is basically advertisements, including editorials. Nowadays, magazines are under pressure to include as many product advertisements as possible, rather than texts and stories. Stop paying for advertisements that try to convince you to spend money.

723. Unsubscribe from junk mail. It reduces the temptation to shop and reduces paper waste too. To unsubscribe from unwanted catalogs, use CatalogChoice.org and DMAChoice.org.

724. Unsubscribe from junk email. Everyone is trying to sell you something. Retailers buy your email address from third-party databases and then send you unsolicited commercial emails. I have friends who have more than 3,000 unread emails in their inboxes. Do you have that many unread emails? Unsubscribe.

725. Cancel subscription boxes. My ex-boyfriend Jared subscribed to Birchbox for $10.00 a month. He loved getting a surprise in the mail every month. He loved the fancy packaging and hoarded all his boxes in his room. He did not even use most of the products, so he technically never got his money's worth. He was crazy. Subscription boxes were his way of justifying spending $10.00 a month for a perceived $30.00 worth of beauty products. Think about it from a business standpoint. Why would companies sell him product samples for $10.00 if they did not make a profit? Samples are free if you just go into the store and ask. You are paying for convenience. Also, the subscription box samples are supposed to entice you enough to buy the full-size product, which means you spend even more money. Instead, spend your money on products you truly love and add value to your life.

726. Think before joining an organization. I used to be a member of Toastmasters International, which is an organization I highly recommend everyone to join. We always had some members who paid for a membership and came back only twice before disappearing. They never got the full value out of their membership. I understand that these days, people have a lot on their plate. There are so many other things you could be doing instead. Think deeply before committing to anything. It is better to join one organization and be fully committed than to join five organizations and be halfhearted. Do not stretch yourself too thin.

727. Read reviews before ever subscribing to anything. I always thought of the Wall Street Journal as a reputable newspaper for finance. Then I read the reviews on Yelp. Wall Street Journal makes it extremely difficult for you to cancel. First, you can only cancel on the phone. Some customer service representatives even make you call back another day. We live in an age where most people have access to the internet. Why can't WSJ just add a cancel link under account settings? Second, WSJ continues charging credit cards after expressing the desire to cancel. Some subscription companies will do anything to make it extremely difficult to cancel, from early termination fees to running you around in circles. Read reviews first.

728. Make a list of all your subscriptions and their renewal dates. Cancel too early, and the companies rob you through hefty termination fees. Cancel too late, and your subscription auto-renews without your permission, sometimes charging you higher prices than the original contract. For instance, Adobe no longer sells traditional licenses for their Creative Suite software. The only way to use Adobe software is by paying a monthly subscription of $29.99 for Creative Cloud. Adobe forces you to pay 50 percent of your remaining contract if you want to cancel early. When it is time to renew, Adobe claims to email customers about the upcoming renewal date, but online reviews claim many customers never receive those emails. The subscription then auto-renewals at $49.99 per month, at which point it is too late. Customers either pay $49.99 every month until the new subscription is almost ending so they can cancel, or they pay the hefty 50 percent of their remaining contract to terminate early.

729. Use Amazon Subscribe & Save. For products that you use regularly, you can receive small discounts. I used Subscribe & Save for iron & vitamin B12 supplements back when I had a nutritional deficiency.

Chapter 20

Gifts and Holidays

Greeting Cards

730. Make your own greeting cards. Hallmark and American Greetings control more than 90 percent of the greeting card market. Also, customers are insensitive to price on special occasions like Valentine's Day. I think greeting cards are expensive. On average, they cost $5.99 each. It is basically a pretty piece of folded cardstock paper that you can make yourself.

731. Purchase $0.99 greeting cards. Customers are averse to cheap greeting cards. People shop with their hearts, not with their logic. At one store, the $0.99 greeting cards were displayed with expensive cards. Customers did not even notice them, so they complained about the high-priced cards. After that, the store created a section specifically for $0.99 greeting cards and added a sign. The store put $5.99 cards in a separate section. Although the cheaper cards were now visible, the expensive cards had a higher percentage increase in sales volume. I read this in 2017 but I can no longer find the article. You don't have to believe me, but I promise it's true!

Gifts

732. Purchase gifts after Christmas. When my sister Jenny was a little girl, she loved Pokémon. Our local Rite Aid sold Pokémon dolls for $15.00 each during the holiday season. I wanted to buy one for her, but I did not want to spend so much for one doll. A few days after Christmas, I walked into Rite Aid to buy something. Lo and behold, the dolls were being sold for $5.00 each. I bought three of them for my sister, and she was so happy.

733. Make your own gifts. HomemadeGiftsMadeEasy.com has a ton of quick, easy, and cheap homemade gift ideas.

734. Make a video. For our one-year anniversary, my husband created a video slideshow from our photos, and he also included a video message at the end. My friend Lingshuang created a dance video for her boyfriend's birthday. Both were free but required time, effort, and creativity.

735. Give the gift of service. Create a gift certificate and offer to babysit, garden, clean the house, prepare a meal, mow the lawn, or give a massage. Be careful about giving certificates for massages. I used to give professional massages and one time I gave my friend Regals a gift certificate for a massage. He never redeemed it because he had a girlfriend. Whoops! I must have made him feel so awkward.

736. Buy discounted gift cards. Sometimes, you can buy gift cards at a discount of up to 35 percent. Look around on the internet to find the best deal for the specific store in mind.

737. Exchange unwanted gift cards. If you receive a gift card for a store you do not shop at, you can exchange it for another store. Visit CardCash.com or CardPool.com to exchange your unwanted gift card.

Gift Wrap

738. Purchase gift packaging after Christmas. Gift packaging is deeply discounted because the demand for them is low after the holiday is over. Save the wrapping paper for next year.

739. Make your own wrapping paper. Find a way to repurpose things you no longer need. For instance, you can turn a cereal box inside out and make a little gift box. You can use maps, sheet music, brown mailing paper, newspaper, leftover fabric, or an old shirt for wrapping gifts. Finish off the gift with a pretty ribbon, measuring tape, wrapping tape, plant leaves, or ink from WiteOut pens. You get the idea.

740. Place your gifts in decorated Mason jars. Mason jars cost only $1.00 when you buy them in bulk. Plus, the gift recipient can always reuse the Mason jar for something else.

Christmas

741. Switch to holding Secret Santa exchanges. Instead of buying one gift for each family member, hold a Secret Santa. Set a budget and have everyone randomly draw a name. Everyone can get the gift that they want. No one goes broke. This could save some families $1,000.00 every year.

742. Buy a fake Christmas tree. When I interviewed my friend Jade about how she handles her household finances with her husband, she shared a few funny stories. In one story that she shared, she said she loved real Christmas trees because of the pine smell. Her husband thought it was a waste of money and wanted to use an artificial tree instead. Jade and her husband reached an agreement: they would alternate every year. The funny part was that Jade set up a real Christmas tree for the past five years. Anyway, on average, a real Christmas tree costs $50.00 and lasts only a few weeks. Real Christmas trees also have the potential to catch fire. Artificial Christmas trees, on the other hand, cost $100.00 and last for ten years. They are even cheaper if you buy right after Christmas. If you use an artificial tree instead of a real tree for the next ten years, you save $400.00.

Chapter 21

Furniture

743. Build your own furniture. I wanted to buy the wall-mounted dropleaf table from Ikea for $39.00. It seemed awfully expensive for a simple table, though, so I made one myself using supplies from the hardware store. I bought 1/2" plywood, two folding shelf brackets, a box of screws and wall anchors, and a quart of white paint. I made the table for under $20.00. There are plenty of DIY furniture projects that you can find online.

744. Buy used furniture. Buy cheap furniture from thrift shops or on Craigslist. Make sure that it is still in good condition and then restore it.

745. Pick up furniture on the sidewalk. When I worked at a spa, my coworker Helen picked up every piece of furniture she came across on the sidewalk. The neighborhood where I worked was Park Slope in Brooklyn, NY. Park Slope was being gentrified at the time, so a lot of residents were moving in and out. Helen picked up used furniture every week!

746. Buy a used mattress. I listed my mattress for sale on Craigslist and then my husband bought it for $40.00. That's how we met. Not only did he get a used mattress at a great price, but he also got me. He found out months later that I slightly lied in my listing. In my listing, I wrote that I slept on the mattress for less than a year. For the record, I was telling the truth. I just forgot to include the fact that I got the mattress used from someone else first. Haha!

747. Cover your mattress with a waterproof mattress pad. I admit that, like a lot of you, I tend to stain my mattress with blood when it is that time of the month. Even as an adult, I once dreamt I was peeing, and then I peed in my bed. Once I start peeing, I can't stop. Don't act like this hasn't happened to you too! Oh, yes, I stained that mattress, and it smelled for days. If you protect your mattress, your mattress will last much longer. Plus, when you want to sell it, you will have an easier time finding a buyer.

748. Sleep on the floor. Forget about buying a bed frame. Sleep on the floor instead. When I first moved out of my parents' house, I bought a trifold mattress on Amazon for $67.99. I slept with my mattress on the floor, and it was extremely comfortable and great for my back. Whenever I needed extra space, I folded up the mattress and stored it away.

749. Bid on furniture at auctions. I once met a couple whose net worth was in the millions. They were extremely frugal, though, especially the wife. They lived in a house worth $300,000.00. The wife furnished the house with antiques from auctions, and she paid very little for everything.

Chapter 22

Love and Relationships

Dating

750. Leave abusive relationships. An abusive partner can manipulate and guilt trip you into spending money. I was in a six-year relationship with a man named Jared. Jared constantly complained about how he could not move out of town for college and have the standard college experience. He got into Macaulay Honors College, which is a commuter school, on a full-ride scholarship and he got a free laptop too. Despite his luck, he was always jealous when he saw what his Facebook friends posted online. Jared's insecurity issues caused him to constantly spend money to feel happy. When I got my first job, he asked me to give him money with a set portion of my paycheck every week so that he could feel happy. I contributed to the "Happy Jared Fund" every week for a whole year and did not think twice about it. Not only did I give him a weekly allowance, I also paid for his duffle coat and restaurant meals. My mom even bought him a $500.00 Vitamix blender. When he upgraded to a new iPhone, he "permanently loaned" me his old iPhone with a cracked screen. One day while rushing to work, I lost it. Jared wanted me to pay him back $100.00 for an iPhone his mom paid for, and he quite clearly was never going to use that phone again after upgrading. Still, he wanted my money. It was only after we broke up and I looked through my expense logbook that I realized how stupid I was. If this is what your partner is like, I am telling you right now to dump that person. You deserve better. You will also never get ahead financially by being with someone like this.

751. Find a romantic partner who is just as frugal as you are. I have no idea how frugal you are. Chances are that if you are reading this book though, you aspire to save money. Having a frugal partner will save you hundreds of thousands of dollars over your lifetime. Many people complain to me about how their spouse just cannot stop spending money. My friend Frank told me his ex-wife bought a designer fur coat without asking first. She told him it cost only $500.00 because it was on sale. A few days later, she admitted that she lied and that it cost $1,000.00. A few days later again, she revealed that the real price was $2,000.00. Do you want to be with someone who spends $2,000.00 on a fur coat without talking to you about it first? Forget about finding some-one who makes a lot of money. Money can always be made. It might just be possible that 20 years from now, your partner gets promoted or has a business and brings home a six-figure income. You never know. Focus on finding someone who can save you a lot of money. If you can find a partner who has similar attitudes about how money should be handled, you will get along much easier and have lower chances of getting divorced. If you cannot find such a partner, you are better off staying single if you care about your financial life. My friend Anthony had a saying: "Stay single, and your pockets will jingle. Get a honey, and you'll have no more money."

752. See whether your potential mate uses credit cards on dates. Credit card use is a sign that your potential mate is not as frugal as you are. Some people pay their credit cards in full every month, but most do not. Leave now before you get too invested and end up forming a relationship. On my first few dates with my husband, I watched to make sure he used cash or debit cards.

753. Have coffee, ice cream, or yogurt for the first date. Coffee and yogurt are cheap dates. I think they are great because they are more conducive for conversations and getting to know one another. Plus, if the chemistry is not there, you have an easy escape plan, and you haven't invested too money on someone you don't have feelings for. My first meeting with my husband was at a fried yogurt place, and I had lots of fun getting to know him.

754. Have dinner at your parents' house on the first date. Someone on *Todd & Jayde's Blown Off* (a radio show on 95.5 PLJ) did this to save money. Her rationale was that if they were going to be together, he might as well have met her parents now to get it over with. Of course, she was blown off. But hey, I took my husband back to my parents' house for dinner after eating fried yogurt, and we still got together. He didn't seem to mind the fact that I wanted to save money.

755. Have a lunch date. Lunch dates are cheaper than dinner.

756. Ladies, order expensive meals on the menu on dates! While feminism has progressed dramatically in the past century and women work full-time just like men, men are still for the most part expected to foot the bill on dates. A great deal of men even insist on it, as it makes them feel masculine.

757. Let the man pay for everything. I know this is totally not feminist. However, some women want the man to pay for everything. If this is you, then go ahead! You get to save your hard-earned money by spending his money instead. My friend Lifi has a hilarious saying: "His money is my money, and my money is my money."

758. Go on cheap dates. AndThenWeSaved.com has a list of 98 super fun and cheap date ideas.

759. Netflix and chill. Great way to spend the night for cheap.

760. Use condoms. Emergency contraceptive pills, abortions, babies, and STD treatments cost money.

761. Buy condoms in bulk. A pack of 3 condoms costs $4.50 at 7Eleven, while a pack of 41 condoms costs $11.84 at Walmart. That is a difference of $1.21 per condom.

762. Make your own sex toys. I found bondage and restraint sex toys selling for $60.00 to $70.00 on AdamEve.com. I could make the same thing with $10.00 worth of sewing supplies and a sewing machine. Get creative and make your own. This tip does not apply to anything that goes inside of your body! Leave that to the professionals.

763. Cohabitate. Even if you and your partner are not married, you can still live together. There is an old saying: "two can live as cheaply as one." You save money by splitting the rent and utilities. Also, since you live together, you do not waste money on transportation to try to see each other. You can also conveniently cook together instead of eating out at restaurants. You also share things around the house (e.g., kitchen supplies, toiletries, furniture, etc.), so you can avoid buying two of each, and you can also take advantage of buying groceries in bulk.

764. Get married. Some people think cohabiting is a good enough substitute for marriage, but when it comes to money, it is not. Most married couples share their finances in deeper and more complex ways that help them build wealth. They pool their finances into a joint bank account. Married couples also benefit from the marital tax deduction, tax-free inheritance, employee health insurance, family leave, and higher capital gains tax exemption on real estate.

765. Try not to get divorced. With divorce rates standing at 50 percent today in the United States, you might as well flip a coin to predict whether a couple will divorce or not. Divorce is expensive. You must pay legal fees. Also, divorce is more than about splitting a couple's assets in half. Divorce can drop a person's net worth by 77 percent. My former chorus teacher has a tough time building wealth even though he got divorced more than 10 years ago. A chunk of his income goes toward paying child support, and at one point, he had to retire, so it wasn't like he could increase his income.

Wedding

766. Get married at city hall. An extravagant wedding is no indicator of whether your marriage will last. A successful marriage depends on whether both spouses are committed enough to make the marriage work and are willing to communicate when resolving conflicts. My parents got married at City Hall in New Zealand after dating for only three months. When exchanging vows, the officiant asked my father where the rings were. My dad didn't even know he had to buy a ring! There was no wedding gown, no ring, no photos, and no party. My parents have been married for 30 years. Many of their friends who had extravagant weddings are now divorced, and some of them even shredded the wedding photos they paid thousands of dollars for. I know several older couples that got married at City Hall and stayed together for decades. They just do not advertise the fact that they never had a wedding, because it does not matter.

767. Have a small, intimate wedding. The average cost of a wedding in the US is $32,641.00! A wedding is only one day long. I would rather take that money and put it towards the down payment for a house. Plan your own wedding, cut down the guest list, and stay on a budget of under $4,000.00.

768. Get married on a weeknight or on Sunday and during the offseason. Just changing the day of the week and the time of the year cuts down the costs significantly. Some couples held their weddings on the week before peak season started, so they had both nice weather and lower prices.

769. Serve a nontraditional wedding cake. You do not have to have a traditional, expensive wedding cake with bland sponge and exotic fillings like guava and mango. One couple ordered ice cream cake from Cold Stone Creamery and all the guests loved it. You can even bake your own cake if you are up for it.

770. Present a fake wedding cake. Another affordable option is to make a fake wedding cake out of cardboard or Styrofoam covered with frosting. The top layer is made of real cake that you can cut. Then when it is time to serve the cake, bring out basic sheet cakes that you can cut and serve.

771. Use fake flowers. Real flowers are expensive and they die. Fake flowers last forever. Buying fake flowers can get a bit expensive too, though. You can learn to make your own out of fabric, crepe paper, or origami paper for a fraction of the regular price.

772. Skip the flowers. Forget about having flowers at all. No one cares. They are there to celebrate your wedding, not to fancy your floral decorations.

773. Find alternatives to bridesmaid bouquets. Bridesmaid bouquets cost from $50.00 to $90.00. Find alternatives. One couple bought lanterns from IKEA for $7.00 each and then spray-painted them and added ribbon to the handles.

774. Have bigger tables. You can purchase fewer centerpieces and tablecloths.

775. Shop for dresses that are not necessarily wedding gowns. The average amount of money spent on a wedding dress in 2020 was $1,631.00. As much as women fantasize about looking like princesses on their special day, spending over a thousand dollars for a dress they wear only once is overkill. And I doubt their daughters would want to wear the same dress at their own wedding. To save money, check out prom dresses and look in department stores. Find a simple dress for under $200.00 and make alternatives for a customized fit. A perfect fit makes all the difference, and will even make the dress look more expensive. If you want, add embellishments like rhinestones, beads, sequins, and lace to make the dress truly a one-of-a-kind.

776. Make your own playlist. Create a playlist that flows, bring your smartphone or computer, and connect it to a sound system. Have a friend be the MC to keep things flowing. Voila, you save $350.00 by not hiring a DJ.

777. Hold your reception at a restaurant. Instead of renting a space and ordering catering, just get married at a fancy restaurant. Everything is already there (e.g., the room, furniture, linens, lighting, beautiful decor, dishes, silverware, fancy display items, etc.). The only things you need to pay for are food and beverage, although some restaurants will charge a fee.

778. Compare between filing your income tax return as married filing jointly vs. married filing separately. There are no hard and fast rules when it comes to this. Each couple is unique. Under certain circumstances, you would save more money by filing jointly. Under others, you save more by filing separately. The best choice also changes year to year. Do your research.

Chapter 23

Pets

779. Own a plant instead of a pet. Pets are expensive. Cats and dogs cost approximately $1,000.00 in the first year and $500.00 every year after. Every time I think about not owning a pet, I think of the plant in the movie Leon the Professional. Leon carried that plant with him everywhere like it was a pet.

780. Own a cheap pet. According to Mint, these are the cheapest pets to own: hermit crabs, geckos, guinea pigs, hamsters, bugs, goldfish, betta fish, birds, chickens, and rats. Since most Americans own cats or dogs, the rest of the tips in this chapter relate to saving money on cat/dog expenses.

781. Adopt from a shelter instead of buying from a breed-er. Adoption costs range from $50.00 to $200.00. Buying a pet from a breeder can cost $500.00 or more.

782. Get a mixed-breed pet instead of pure. Mixed-breed pets live longer and have lower vet bills. Many purebred pets develop health problems.

783. Buy the healthiest brand of pet food. Veterinary care is expensive. You pay more now for healthier food, but you save money in the long term by preventing as many health issues as possible. To save a bit of money, go on the food brand's website and see whether there are any coupons you can print out.

784. Buy pet food in bulk and split the cost with a friend. The larger the bag of pet food, the lower the unit cost. Pet foods have a shelf life, so split it with a friend. That way, you save money, and your pet finishes all the food before it expires.

785. Exercise your pet every day. Just like humans, pets need exercise to maintain a healthy lifestyle. The healthier your pet, the less you pay for veterinary care in the future.

786. Brush your pet's teeth using pet toothpaste every day. Dental disease can affect pets too. Dental tartar builds up and damages gums. The bacteria in the tartar can enter the bloodstream and affect the heart, lungs, and kidneys. Take preventative measures.

787. Groom at home. You can save as much as $500.00 a year by grooming your pet at home.

788. Make your own pet toys. There are tons of DIY pet toy ideas on the internet. They are usually cheap and easy to make and made from things around the house.

789. Buy durable collars, leashes, and id tags. Buy things that will last for years to come. That way, you won't have to constantly replace them.

790. Spay or neuter your pet. Spayed female pets live longer and healthier. Spaying also prevents breast tumors and uterine infections. Neutering male pets prevents testicular cancer and prostate problems. Low-cost clinics charge less than $200.00 for spaying or neutering.

791. Avoid pet insurance. The expensive premiums are not worth it. In the game of insurance, the insurance companies will, statistically, always win. The companies will always collect more money in premiums than in benefits they pay out. Most people buy pet insurance when their pets are young and monthly premiums are at their lowest. The premium will only go up from there through age-based price hikes, causing the average policy holder to only have insurance for three years, not for the life of the pet. You are better off shopping around for veterinary services. But anyway, if you're not comfortable forgoing insurance, buy insurance for now and continue to build your emergency fund. When you get to the point where you have such a large emergency fund that covering the medical costs for accidents and illnesses don't sting as much, you can drop insurance. If you want to read more before deciding on pet insurance, you can read "Is Pet Insurance Worth It" by Jeff Blyskal on The Washington Post (Blyskal, 2018).

792. Walk your dog yourself. Quit wasting money on a dog walker.

Chapter 24

Music and Technology

Technology

793. Purchase expensive technological devices and gadgets in states with no sales tax. When buying an expensive electronic, try buying it in Alaska, Delaware, Montana, Oregon, and New Hampshire. Either ask a friend who lives in one of these states to buy it for you or buy it while you are on a road trip. Sales tax makes all the difference on items retailing over $1,500.00.

794. Shop online. When it comes to technology, online retailers tend to offer lower prices than brick-and-mortar stores.

795. Skip the extended warranty. It's overpriced and a total waste of money. Only buy it if you are a total klutz who is prone to breaking everything.

796. Read the reviews before buying any technology. More expensive electronics are not necessarily better. Read in-depth reviews before buying. You want to get good value for your money.

Televisions

797. Avoid buying a smart TV. Smart TVs are more expensive, and they also pose a security risk, as they connect to the internet. People can use smart TV cameras to spy on you in your own home, and the TV companies monitor what you watch to give you targeted ads. The main purpose of a TV is to display images on the screen, so just buy a regular TV.

798. Buy an older model TV. They tend to be cheaper and deeply discounted, as manufacturers have stopped manufacturing them. Pick a size as big as you want, preferably the biggest one that will fit in your room.

799. Avoid buying a 4k TV. If you already have one, then fine. If you don't, then don't buy one. They are expensive and lack standardization too. Also, very few movies, TV shows and live broadcasts are being released in 4K. Few Blu-ray players support 4K TV, and the ones that do support 4K TV are not cheap.

800. Create a home theater. This is expensive at first, but you save a lot of money long-term. Since movie theater tickets and popcorn are so expensive nowadays, you might as well watch movies at home. For example, a family of four pays $50.00 to watch a new movie at the theater ($12.50 per person). Add on two bags of popcorn for $13.00 ($6.50 per bag). Assuming the family frequents the movie theater twice a month, that's $1,512.00 per year! Create a home theater, subscribe to Netflix, and make your own popcorn. After one year, you'll recoup the costs.

801. Avoid buying cables in stores. HDMI cables shouldn't cost more than $5.00, but a lot of stores charge $20.00. Buy it on Amazon or on Monoprice instead.

Computers

802. Buy an older model computer. New models are faster and more efficient, but depending on your needs, you might not need the latest model. See if a slightly older model is good enough for your expectations.

803. Buy an open box or refurbished computer. Many people buy a new computer, take it home, open the box, find something they don't like about it, and then return it. Many manufacturers repair the computers until they are like new and then the retailers resell these computers with a significant discount. Only about 5 percent of refurbished products are defective. When buying a refurbished computer, know the return policy and the warranty period, and buy brands you trust.

804. Identify your computing needs. Make a list of what you will use the computer for and then research your options. Do you need it for gaming, for downloading music and movies, for designing graphics, or for simple browsing and basic tasks? For the latter, you do not need to spend so much money—any computer model will work. My friend boasts about having the latest computers, but he rarely uses computers and when he does, he never does anything beyond basic tasks. There's just no need to spend that much. His money could be better spent elsewhere.

805. Buy computers in the late summer or early fall. During that time of the year, college students are returning to school, so there might be huge sales.

806. Cover your computer keyboards. When I was a kid, my dad bought me a brand-new Dell laptop. After two years, I had to beg for a new laptop because I always ate food while using my laptop. Lots of food particles and dust got caught under the keyboard gaps. I did get a new laptop, but the same thing happened again. I know—Annie Yang is such a slob. Anyway, I finally got smart and used a keyboard cover the moment I bought a new laptop. If you keep your computers clean and well-maintained, you don't need to upgrade as often.

807. Cover your laptops with a case. I am very careful when taking care of my laptop today because I paid for it with my hard-earned money instead of asking my dad to pay. I have a MacBook Pro (13-inch, Early 2011). After six years, this laptop is still going strong. I cover it with a hardshell case to prevent scratches. I even cover the palm rest and the trackpad with an aluminum-colored protector. This prevents grease and sweat from harming my Mac-Book Pro. Whenever I take my laptop outside, I put it in a well-padded bag or sleeve. I am very protective of my baby, as a new one costs at least $1,299.00 plus sales tax. Update: I took really good care of my MacBook but it died in 2017 at six years old due to hardware failure, and Apple considered it "vintage" and would not repair. I really liked Apple computers back then but not anymore, because the parts nowadays are all soldered in instead of screwed in to make them more lightweight and compact. This makes repairs more expensive, so I'm a Windows gal now.

808. Upgrade your current computer. It is possible you do not need to buy a new computer. You can upgrade your desktop computer or laptop with new parts.

809. Wait before upgrading your computer. My ex-boyfriend Jared always had to have the latest and greatest when it came to his MacBook Pro. Back in 2012, he upgraded his hard drive to an SSD for more than $300.00. He did not care that much about the price because it was his mom's money. Over the years, the market prices for SSDs have plummeted.

810. Do the upgrades yourself. I wanted to change the battery on my MacBook Pro, so I called my local Apple store and asked them how much it would cost. They told me to buy the battery on MacSales.com for $99.00 and then come in to have it serviced for $129.00. I thought paying $228.00 in total to change the battery was awfully expensive. Instead, I bought a new battery for $69.23 and Samsung 850 EVO 250GB SSD for $100.98 on Amazon. Then I asked my husband to do it for me. He watched instruction videos on YouTube and did it. It was straightforward. This whole process cost me only $170.21—much less than going to Apple. Thank you to my husband! You're the best!

811. Shop around for the best price if you do not want to do the upgrades yourself. Going back to the manufacturer for repair or upgrade is not always the best route. When my friend Michelle cracked her iPhone 6S screen, she brought it to Apple for repair for $150.00. It took one week to get her phone back. When I saw it, the first thing I noticed about her phone was how dim her screen looked. The brightest display setting was unusually dark compared to my iPhone on the same setting. We took it to a local electronic repair shop. They popped Michelle's phone open and saw that the new screen was not a genuine Apple product. The business owner was willing to replace her phone with a genuine Apple screen for $75.00. Plus, it would be done in under an hour, right in front of us.

Software

812. Use less cloud storage. As an example, I pay $50.00 per year for a custom email address using my own domain name. The package comes with 30 GB cloud storage on Google Drive. Honestly, even with the package, I use only 4 GB of cloud storage, which is well under the limit of Google's 15 GB free storage limit. As another example, my iPhone SE has 16 GB of storage, and I only use 7.13 GB. How do I do it? I disabled iCloud Photo Library. Instead, I regularly transfer my photos to my computer, back them up on Google Drive, and then delete them from my phone. I refuse to pay $0.99 per month for iCloud storage.

813. Use PortableApps.com. The apps on this site are free, legal, and safe. Moreover, they are portable, as in you can take the software with you on any portable storage device (USB flash drive, external hard drive, memory card, etc.) or cloud drive (DropBox, Google Drive, iCloud, etc.). I used Photoshop Portable CS6 when it was still available for download on the site. The software was just as good as the original full version.

814. Use open-source software. They are free to use. Also, many of the most popular software are used by millions of people (e.g., Linux, Mozilla Firefox, WordPress, OpenOffice, GIMP, VLC Media Player, etc.).

815. Design your own website. Nowadays, sites like Wix.com and SquareSpace.com make it easy to make your own website.

816. Download AdBlock on your web browser. Ad servers track you and gather your personal information. Your personal information is used to sell you more targeted ads. Download Ad-Block so you can stop spending your hard-earned money on ad-promoted consumerism. Another benefit of AdBlock is that it helps you conserve your mobile data, especially when visiting news sites where more than half your data gets eaten up by ads.

Music

817. Purchase used music instruments and equipment. Quality musical instruments are designed to last a lifetime. When buying a musical instrument, ask why it is being sold, how old it is, whether it had any repairs, whether it has any issues, and whether it comes with the case. If possible, buy it in person so you can try playing with it before buying. When I was a teenager, my mother bought me a brand-new acoustic-electric guitar for $350.00. When I got bored of my guitar-playing hobby, I sold it for only $100.00. The guitar was still in great condition—I just wanted to make space in my room for other things. I learned my lesson: buy a secondhand guitar in the future. Look on Craigslist. You will find many secondhand musical instruments at low prices.

818. Listen to music on YouTube. I admit that I'm not a huge music fan. My husband loves music and downloads the highest quality songs he can. Since I don't care as much, I am okay with listening to music on YouTube. I am sure many of the unofficial music videos on YouTube violate copyright laws. However, many music recording companies upload their copyrighted videos on VEVO for people to watch and listen to.

819. Stream music on Spotify or Pandora. They offer free plans and premium plans for $9.99 per month. Spotify offers a 50 percent discount for students enrolled in an accredited college or university.

Cameras and Photos

820. Buy older model camera gear. You do not need the latest and greatest. Last year's model works just fine.

821. Make your own camera accessories. My friend Lingshuang and I once made a camera stabilizer using pipe, wood, weights, screws, and paint for under ten dollars. If you bought the tripod, it would cost close to $100.00. I've seen people make their own reflectors, diffusers, and light boxes. You name it, and someone has most likely made it before. Photography and filmmaking are expensive hobbies, so people are always looking for ways to cut costs.

822. Only buy camera gear that you need. Do not buy gear just because it sounds cool. Buy it because you need it to fill a specific purpose.

823. Borrow cameras and camera gear from friends. One time, I had to give a speech and wanted to record it. Obviously, I did not want to spend hundreds of dollars on this, so I borrowed my friend Lingshuang's camera and tripod. You could do the same if you only need a camera once.

824. Rent camera gear for one-time projects or assignments. Not only do you save money, but you also get to try before you buy.

825. Purchase used DSLR cameras and camera gear. Unless you are a professional photographer, in general, you should purchase used. Be sure to inspect the item before buying. You will save from 25 to 50 percent of the original price.

826. Buy off-brand for camera lenses and batteries. The main brands are Canon and Nikon. There are other reputable manufacturers that produce top-notch lenses for lower prices. Off-brand batteries do not hold their charge as long, but for the price, you can buy multiple batteries. Just do not skimp on memory cards! Buy SanDisk or Lexar, as you want to keep your precious photos.

827. Sell your old gear. As you buy more gear, your old gear goes unused and starts collecting dust. Sell it sooner than later, as your camera gear loses value the older it gets.

828. Use a photo printing service rather than printing at home. If you print photos at home, you need to buy a photo printer, printer cartridges, and blank photo paper. Printing photos at home is convenient, but the costs add up quickly. Best to wait until you can use a service. At some places, you can get great prints for $0.10 to $0.15 per print.

829. Keep your photos in digital form instead of printing. This fits in with the philosophy of going completely paperless. Nowadays, people take photos 247. Just look at Instagram and Snapchat. Photos aren't as rare as they used to be. You can choose to only print photos of special moments (e.g., birthdays, holidays, vacations, graduation ceremonies, award ceremonies, weddings, anniversaries, etc.).

Printing

830. Go paperless. Keep your statements, order confirmations, and documents in digital format instead of printing. Email PDF documents to colleagues instead of faxing.

831. Print less. I found this was much easier to do after I graduated from school. I no longer needed to print multiple-page essays and assignments. I used to print at home when I was a student. Now that I don't need to print as much, I don't own a printer. On the rare occasions when I do need to print, I go to FedEx or Staples or my local public library.

832. Use two printers if you print at home. Use an efficient and inexpensive laser printer for everyday printing. Use a quality inkjet printer for higher-quality prints. This saves money on expensive ink cartridges.

833. Purchase compatible off-brand ink and toner cartridges. They meet the same performance standards as cartridges from the original manufacturer, but they cost much less.

834. Use Ecofont Vera Sans as your go-to typeface when printing at home. This typeface punches a bunch of tiny holes in each letter to help you save 28 percent on ink. It is free to download and use.

835. Print in grayscale. Unless you are printing a formal document or a document for a client/customer, grayscale is good enough. This cuts back on the usage of color ink. When using self-service copy machines at FedEx or Staples, double-check the settings. I often find that their machines are set to print in color by default. Many times, the document I need to print is already in black and white. Printing in color could cost me five times more for the same exact result.

836. Decrease page margins and line spacing. You can fit more lines on each sheet and save paper.

837. Proofread before printing. Check your work before printing. As a student, I had to reprint many documents after finding errors in my original print. My dad and my sister complained I was constantly printing.

838. Print on both sides of a sheet of paper. You save money on paper. This only works if you print at home. If you print at a self-service kiosk, you get charged the same regardless.

839. Print at school if you are a student. When I attended Kingsborough Community College for my associate degree, I had access to free printing in the computer lab. The limit was 1,100 sheets of paper, which renewed every semester. I printed a lot of paper! I always used the stapler on the computer lab desk. Soon the employee behind the desk knew me as the "Stapler Girl."

Chapter 25

Entertainment

840. Choose your friends wisely. I taught a personal finance workshop to college students and asked everyone what they spent their money on. A student named David told me he could easily spend $150.00 per night hanging out with his friends at the bar. He did not have an alcohol addiction, so why did he spend so much money without realizing it? To him, he was spending time with his friends, and the money was an afterthought. Either find a new way to hang out with your friends or make new friends.

841. Learn self-massage. I used to give professional massages. At the place where I worked, we had clients come in for a massage every week! The national average for a one-hour massage costs $60.00/hour, and that does not include tips. I cannot imagine paying $240.00 + tips every month for weekly massages. Massage yourself for free instead.

842. Exchange massages with your partner. This is even better than self-massage because you get to bond with your partner.

843. Attend free public library events. I used to live in New York City. I must tell you… the New York Public Library system is massive. There is an event for everyone, both suited for a variety of ages and a variety of interests. At the time of this writing, they have 6,904 events scheduled for the near future. Right now, I live in Boston, MA. Boston Public Library also holds many free events. It used to have knitting classes, nerd meets, story time, family LEGO nights, movie showings, and more. Check to see what events your local public library offers, but things are complicated now with the COVID-19 pandemic.

844. Attend free community events. Many cities and towns have an official Convention & Visitors Bureau to promote tourism. Go on the official website for your city and see what events are happening in your area. For example, in Lubbock, there are live music and shows, sports, cultural events, exhibits, festivals, holiday-related events, and seminars.

845. Stomp on autumn leaves. When I was a kid, I loved stomping on a pile of raked leaves because of the crunching sound. Adults can do this too. I think too many adults lose their childlike wonder and their playfulness. (If you live in Lubbock though, forget about it. The only things here for you to stomp on are tumbleweeds.)

846. Invite your friends over for coffee, tea, or a meal in your home. It is hard connecting with people in coffee shops and restaurants. Coffee shops, restaurants, and other public places are not ideal places for you and your friends to be open and vulnerable. If you invite people over to your home instead, you will save money and find your relationships grow deeper faster.

847. Say no to social events, or agree to meet after dinner. Back when I had my first full-time job and got paid peanuts for my work, I said no to pretty much every social invitation. I wanted to save money even though it meant turning down the chance to have fun with my friends.

848. Avoid going to the mall. When you go to the mall, you spend money even if you did not intend to. Everywhere you look, there is something to spend your money on. If you need to go to the mall, then buy what you need and leave immediately.

849. Go ice-skating. When I was a teenager, my friends and I went to the Sky Rink at Chelsea Piers NYC. Each person had to pay $17.00. I found out later that ice-skating in Bryant Park was free if you brought your own skates. Sure, waiting in line took forever, but it was free!

850. Turn your hobby into a business. Almost anything you do can be turned into a business. If you do not want to make a profit, then at least sell items or services for the cost you got the materials for. That way, you can enjoy your hobby without paying for it.

851. Have a hobby that does not involve collecting. My friend Chung told me that he liked to collect fish, but his wife always got mad at him whenever he added a new fish to his collection. I thought nothing of it until he told me that he once spent $10,000.00 on a rare fish that ended up dying a year later. No wonder his wife was always mad. My dad enjoys collecting stamps and he has tons of boxes of stamps in his home. Not only are the stamps expensive, they also take up too much space in the house. If he had any more, then he and my mom would have to move to a bigger place and pay more in rent. Folks, collecting is an expensive hobby.

852. Eat ice cream at the local gelato shop. Cheap and yummy.

853. Have a no-spend weekend. Try to not spend any money for an entire weekend. This means no eating out, shopping, or ordering things online.

854. Volunteer for a cause. When you volunteer, you make a difference and improve your community. You also meet new people, gain experiences, build your resume, and feel great.

855. Sell handmade items on Etsy. If you're crafty, you can turn your knitting, sewing, jewelry making, painting, or photography hobby into an online business.

856. Attend events at your local university. Colleges often have free events that are open to the public. When I lived in New York City, I often attended events at Macaulay Honors College, even though I wasn't even a college student. I went to the annual CUNY Film Festival and even went to the Spring Formal. At that point in my life, I refused to go to college, but I still wanted to make friends who were closer to my age. Being at these events was a great way to network.

857. If you're a college student, use the school's gym. Lots of college students gain weight when they live away from their parents because of the unhealthy food that's widely available. Universities charge around $100.00 per semester for a membership at their recreation center. It is totally worth it if you go on a regular basis. Not only do you stay fit, you make friends there too.

858. Spend a sunny day at the pool. When I'm bored, I go to the Student Leisure Pool at Texas Tech University. The Leisure Pool has a 645ft. lazy river and a hot tub too. It's amazing. I'm not a Texas Tech student, but if I go with a student or faculty member, I can get in by paying the $10.00 daily guest fee. You don't necessarily need to do what I did. If you can find a public pool in your area, go for it.

859. Workout at your local park's playground. When I was a kid, my dad paid me $5.00 per day to play on the monkey bars and to climb up the sliding pole. He thought defying gravity would make me grow taller. Now that I look back as an adult, this was a good way to encourage exercise. As an adult, you can use the monkey bars to do pullups and leg lifts. You can also climb up the sliding pole. You'll be surprised by how much strength you'll need to get your body off the ground. Many parks also have a trail that you can run around.

860. Watch the sunrise or sunset. This is free! Just find some place where you can see the horizon.

861. Call friends you have not spoken to in a while. I admit this one is awkward. While I shouldn't be scared to call my friends to stay in touch, I do feel that way. I'm scared it's been so long since we spoke that we have grown apart. I tried this today with a friend I haven't called in a year, and she didn't seem interested at all. If you want to stay friends, you must actively maintain your friendships. Make that damn phone call already.

862. Go fishing on fish-for-free days. My mom used to fish her own fish. The fish tasted fresh and delicious. Seafood is expensive, but fishing is free.

863. Do household chores. A clean home equals a clear mind.

864. Build a giant blanket fort. This is great if you have kids. When I was younger, my cousin and I built a giant fort using chairs, blankets, and tables. We would hide inside and play games.

865. Take a free online class. The internet has made free education so accessible. There are plenty of websites where you can learn for free: Coursera, Udacity, CodeAcademy, Udemy, Open2Study, and Alison.

866. Watch movies using movie tickets purchased from Costco. Costco sells movie tickets for AMC, Regal, and Cinemark, but they're all in 10packs. Still, the individual movie tickets end up costing between $8.50 and $9.00 when you buy in bulk. In New York City and other large cities, this is totally worth it because a movie ticket now costs at least $15.00 no matter which theater you go to. If you live in a town like Lubbock, don't follow my advice because movie tickets here cost only $6.00, surprisingly.

867. Go to a matinee showing of a movie. Most people prefer watching movies in the evening. Thus, movie theaters charge lower prices for matinee showings to attract customers during the day. It's the same movie—just at an earlier time in the day. I remember when my friends and I went to watch *The Conjuring* at AMC. It was the matinee showing, which costs only $8.00. I gave the cashier a movie ticket I got from Costco for $8.50, which meant I paid 50 cents more than I had to. I felt so stupid. Don't do that.

868. Watch movies on discount days. Some small movie theaters like to have discount days to attract more customers. I know Kent Theater in Brooklyn, NY charged $5.00 for all tickets on Wednesdays. That's a great deal you won't find anywhere else!

869. Eat at home before watching movies at the cinema. Movie theaters have an 85 percent profit margin on concessions. According to Movie Food Prices, at AMC, 1 large popcorn + 1 large drink combo costs $15.99, and at Cinemark, the same thing costs $14.95. This is very expensive. Plus, you won't even feel full with a bag of popcorn and a drink. As a kid, when I went to watch movies with my friends, my mom forced me to eat at home beforehand. I felt left out, but I understand now that she saved us a lot of money.

870. Have a picnic. Invite a bunch of friends to the park on a hot, sunny day. Bring casual foods (preferably foods that can be eaten without utensils), ice, drinks, condiments, salt and pepper, cups, plates, utensils, napkins, paper towels, a large blanket, and a basket. According to the American Farm Bureau, the average picnic costs only $6.00 per person.

871. Borrow DVDs from the library. The library isn't only a place for books. More people borrow DVDs from libraries than from Netflix. According to Consumerist, public libraries loan out 2.1 million DVDs daily for free. Meanwhile, Netflix loans out 2 million daily for $7.99 per month in addition to their streaming service plans.

872. Rent DVDs from Red Box. If your library does not offer the DVDs you want to watch, then you can rent from Red Box. It costs $1.50 per day so long as you return the DVD before 9:00 PM. If you return after 9:00 PM, then you will be charged for an additional day. Red Box is worth it if you plan to rent five or fewer DVDs per month. Otherwise, you should pay for a Netflix subscription instead.

873. Play video games. Video games are expensive—new games cost around $60.00. Save money by refusing to buy new games right at the release. Instead, buy used video games after the hype has died down. If you insist on buying new video games, then sell them when you are done.

874. Play board games. I used to think board games were for kids, but there are adult board games too. Board games help people socialize by giving them something to talk about and board games break down social barriers. A few minutes into a board game, strangers become comfortable with each other because they play around and tease each other. The average board game costs $30.00, and it can always be reused. Invite friends over for pizza and share the costs. The average pizza pie ranges from $8.90 to $16.00 depending on where you live.

875. Play chess. Chess develops memory and logical thinking and improves concentration. Chess encourages you to be imaginative and creative because you need to plan possible combinations and predict actions. Lower quality chess sets cost $10.00. If you want a higher quality wooden chess set, expect to pay more than $30.00.

876. Play card games. Card games are fun, keep your mind sharp, and improve your gross and fine motor skills. A pack of cards is cheap and portable. Plus, card games can be played any-where, so long as there is a flat surface.

877. Solve puzzles. Puzzles improve IQ, cognitive ability, concentration, motor skills, problem-solving skills, and productiv-ity. Some popular puzzles are jigsaw puzzles, 3D wooden brainteaser puzzles, Sudoku, and Rubik's cubes are common puz-zles. Most adult puzzles I find on Amazon cost under $15.00.

878. Go hiking. There are so many health benefits to hiking. Hiking improves your cardiorespiratory and muscular fitness. It lowers your risk of heart disease, stroke, high blood pressure, high cholesterol, colon cancer, and breast cancer. It reduces depres-sion, improves sleep quality, and controls weight. Hiking exercises every part of your body. The first time I ever went hiking, my en-tire body was sore for the next two days. Carpool with a group of friends to a national park and share the gas money. Bring lots of water and some snacks. The best thing about going with a group of friends is that you'll have long and deep conversations.

879. Attend community theatre. Community theatre is thea-ter that is made by a community for a community. Tickets prices at Lubbock Community Theatre are between $15.00 and $25.00. Student rush tickets are only $5.00. These prices are very afforda-ble compared to professional theatre.

880. Use discount codes when buying Broadway tickets. Discounts range between 20 to 60 percent off the face-value price. Find the codes by visiting PlayBill.com, TheaterMania.com, and BroadwayBox.com. Using the sites is free, but they ask for personal information. For people living in New York City, you can use NYTix.com for discounts on orchestra and mezzanine seats. The website has a page that lets you see whether discounts are currently available for the show you want to watch. To get the discount, you need to pay $4.00 for 30 days of access to the discount guide. The access does not auto-renew, so you do not have to worry about canceling.

881. Buy Broadway tickets directly at the box office. This will save you money on Telecharge or Ticketmaster service fees, which cost about $10.00 per ticket. You can also use discount codes at the box office.

882. Write your bucket list. Fitzhugh Dodson said, "goals that are not written down are just wishes." A bucket list gives you direction in life, helps you stay focused on your goals, and makes you reflect on your purpose. Grab a pen and a sheet of paper. Then write down a list of 100 things you want to do, places you want to go, and people you want to meet before you die (or, kick the bucket).

883. Go bowling. If you are a serious bowler who bowls faster, then you can save money by renting a lane by the hour. If you are bowling with friends as a social event, then you are better off paying per game. This way, you can eat, drink, and talk without worrying about getting the full value of your money. Bowling alleys also offer weekly specials. For example, at my local bowling alley, on Fridays and Saturdays, the prices are $10.00 per person for two hours of unlimited games, and it includes shoe rental. On Sundays, the price is $2.00 per game and $3.75 for shoe rental. On weekdays, the prices are even cheaper to attract customers on slow days.

884. Listen to podcasts. Podcasts are free and they cover a wide variety of topics. Podcasts are also one of the best ways to learn and be entertained while doing something else. Listen to podcasts while getting ready in the morning, while commuting to and from work, while waiting in line, while going on a walk, while doing household chores, or while preparing meals.

885. Learn to juggle. Juggling sharpens your focus and concentration, relieves stress, increases the range of motion of your arms and shoulders, improves coordination, and burns calories. The best thing about juggling is that you can do it anywhere, and anyone can do it regardless of age and body type. Juggling is also cheap—you can buy a set of juggling balls for under $10.00 on Amazon. Of course, if you want higher quality juggling balls, then you'll need to pay a bit more.

886. Bake a loaf of homemade bread. Fresh bread straight from the oven smells wonderful and tastes delicious. When you make your own bread, you know for sure there are no weird additives or chemicals in your bread. You can choose the types of flour you want to use. You can add your choice of seeds, nuts, dried fruits, and herbs. You can express your creativity by forming your own shapes. Kneading dough is also a therapeutic activity. Baking homemade bread can be a form of family bonding. Baking your own bread costs around the same as store bought white bread ($1.00). However, you should be comparing the cost to artisan bread, not to Wonder Bread, because essentially that's what you are making. Baking your own bread is cheaper than buying artisan bread, such as wholewheat, long fermented sourdough, sprouted grain bread, and gluten-free bread. These loaves of bread cost between $2.00 and $7.00 per loaf when you buy them at the grocery store.

887. Meet your neighbors. Most Americans do not know their neighbors. Say hi to your neighbors, find out their names, and interact with them. Neighbors will help watch your house when you are away, collect mail when it accumulates, lend you tools, invite you to parties, accept packages when no one is home, pet sit and watch your kids. You can meet your neighbors by knocking on their doors and introducing yourself or by joining NextDoor.com.

888. Start a blog. Write on a topic that interests you or on something you want to learn more about to track your progress toward a goal. Blogging will make you a better writer and a better thinker. By starting a blog, you get to meet new people and inspire others. Start a free blog on Wordpress.com or Blogger.com. After you try blogging, and you're sure you want to expand your blog, purchase a domain name and hosting service.

889. Write your will. The only thing that is guaranteed in life is death. Though this is an unpleasant thought... you might die tomorrow, so write your will soon. Lawyers typically charge $1,000.00 for writing a will. If your situation is very straightforward (e.g., leaving everything to one person), then you can draft your own will. You can purchase forms and guides for a basic will from LegalZoom.com or Nolo.com. Creating your own will online costs from $20.00 to $100.00. Ask a lawyer to review the will for a small fee. Have an independent witness sign the document and get it notarized. Voila!

890. Learn to knit. Knitting is a therapeutic hobby that re du-ces stress and anxiety. Knitting also improves hand-eye coordina-tion. There are also knitting groups you can join, making knitting a social experience too. Depending on the type of yarn you are using, knitting can cost as low as $5.00 for a scarf or as much as $100.00 when using more expensive yarns like pure cashmere.

891. Organize a potluck party. Hosting a potluck is an easy way to gather friends together without all the stress. People can build community by eating together more often. Many people nowadays have specific food preferences, such as vegetarian, ve-gan, and gluten-free. Potlucks are good in that there is no need to plan a menu. Say to guests, "Make something you eat!" Also, with potlucks, everyone can try a variety of dishes.

892. Go on a walking tour in your city. Many cities have free walking tours (well, not completely free because they ask for donations at the end). It is a great way to learn more about your city. When I visited Boston, I went on a free walking tour of the Freedom Trail. The tour guide was hilarious and I learned interesting facts about the local businesses along the Freedom Trail. Free walking tours may only be available in larger cities. In a city like Lubbock, there is no way to get around the city without a car.

893. Practice origami. Origami is a portable hobby that you can practice anywhere. Since it is a mentally stimulating activity that requires your concentration, it can help you get your mind off whatever is bothering you now. It is also artistic. Origami paper is sold in packs, which means one sheet comes out to cost only around 6 cents.

894. Visit museums when they have free admission. Museums are an informal learning environment that can expose you to in-depth information on a subject. They appeal to visual, audio, and kinesthetic learning styles. Some museums are completely free. For example, all Smithsonian Museums in Washington, D.C., are free. The only one that is not free is the African American History and Culture Museum, which opened in 2016. Several museums have free admission during certain days or certain times of the day. Some museums have suggested general admission, but many people don't understand that it's donation based. For example, the American Museum of Natural History has a suggested general admission of $22.00 for adults, but you can donate $1.00 for admission if you want.

895. Visit the zoo when it is free. Zoo tickets are expensive. At the Bronx Zoo in New York City, an adult ticket costs $36.95. No one goes to the zoo alone, obviously. Let's say you go with your spouse. You could easily pay $73.90 just to explore for one day. Don't forget that the food sold inside the zoo is expensive too. Thankfully, the Bronx Zoo offers pay-what-you-wish donation for general admission on Wednesdays. Pay $1.00 and explore the zoo. See if your local zoo has something similar.

896. Visit historical sites. Old towns and cities will have cathedrals, palaces, old forts, and town halls that you can visit. Most have free entry or inexpensive admission prices. If you insist on not paying, you can admire the exterior architecture and take some nice pictures.

897. Learn the basics of a new topic using OpenCourseWare. OpenCourseWare is university courses offered online for free via the internet. OpenCourseWare does not lead to a college degree or offer access to faculty, so it is great for self-learners who want education for personal benefits. Check out MIT OpenCourseWare and The Open University OpenLearn.

898. Plan next month's budget. I like to do this approximately five days before the new month begins.

899. Update your financial spreadsheets. I like to track my expenses every day and update my monthly budget every few days. Budgets should be flexible, not set in stone. Take time to adjust your budget after the new month has started.

900. Calculate your net worth. List your assets, list your liabilities, and then subtract your liabilities from your assets to determine your net worth. Calculate your net worth periodically. Finding out your net worth can be a wakeup call to let you know that you're completely off track. On the other hand, if you're doing well, your net worth lets you know that you are progressing.

901. Calculate your total lifetime earnings. Request a Statement of Earnings from the Social Security Administration. Add on to this number an estimate of all the childhood allowances, monetary gifts, and other income you never filed taxes for. You'll be shocked to see how high it is. Knowing this number can be a wakeup call. You'll ask yourself, where did all the money go? Stop spending your money on meaningless stuff.

902. Watch YouTube videos. YouTube videos can be informative and educational, or they can be funny and entertaining. Plus, it is free!

903. Start a YouTube channel. Many people like watching YouTube videos, but never make their own. Forget about the potential to monetize your YouTube channel. Starting your own channel allows you to share viewpoints that you feel others need to hear, to share what you know, and to connect with new people online. Making videos can be as cheap or as expensive as you want it to be.

904. Watch TED talks. TED talks are inspiring, entertaining, interesting, and free. TED talks cover a wide breadth of topics, so they will improve your general knowledge. You will think about ideas from a different perspective. Visit TED.com today!

905. Join Toastmasters International. Toastmasters International is a nonprofit organization that will improve your communication, public speaking, and leadership skills. After my ex-boyfriend Jared broke up with me in 2015, my life reached its lowest point. I did not want to engage in any destructive behaviors, so I joined a local Toastmasters club. My life made a 180-degree turn. It boosted my self-confidence and I made supportive friends who lifted me up again. New members pay a onetime $20.00 fee and all members pay $45.00 international dues every six months. This costs less than a gym membership and the value you get out of this organization is tremendous.

906. Give a TEDx talk. All you need is a fresh idea worth sharing and an 18minute talk. You do not have to be invited. You can apply.

907. Practice yoga. Yoga improves flexibility, builds muscle strength, increases blood flow, and perfects your posture. Perfect posture exudes confidence. To be honest, yoga in the United States is overpriced. You do not need expensive Lululemon pants or $100.00 monthly memberships to practice yoga. When I was 18 years old, I wanted to learn yoga, but I did not have the money to pay for the $80.00 per month membership at my local studio. I asked whether I could pay per class and they told me no. Low on cash, I bought a yoga mat for $20.00 and a used book titled *Richard Hittleman's Yoga: 28 Day Exercise Plan* for $4.74 on Amazon. I taught myself yoga using this book and practiced the routines for the past four years. I have excellent flexibility and would be placed in an advanced level class if I did choose to take classes.

908. Scan your old pictures. I grew up during a time when most cameras used film and photos had to be printed at the local lab. I have hundreds of photos from my childhood. Before moving out of my parents' house, I wanted to scan these photos to have a digital copy. I downloaded the Heirloom App on my iPhone (free) and then I spent a couple of weekends scanning photographs. There is simply no need to pay a lot of money for a flatbed scanner.

909. Email professional contacts to build or maintain your network. It is not what you know, but whom you know. Eighty percent of jobs are filled through networking. People in your network will help you if you help them. See how you can help people, help them, and watch them reciprocate. Some people might never reciprocate. Some people might reciprocate years later. That does not matter; do not keep score. Just get your name out there and build your reputation.

910. Read a book. Reading makes you focused, smart, interesting, attractive, and creative. Twenty-seven percent of Americans did not read a single book in 2015. Do not fall into this category. Cultivate a reading habit and read a book for at least 15 minutes per day.

911. Write a book. There are plenty of good reasons to write a book, such as helping others, building a business, switching careers, and establishing authority. By writing a book, people perceive you as an expert and you increase your value. Do not write a book to become a famous, bestselling author and to sell millions of books. Most authors never sell millions. They make money selling other things while using the book to market their credibility. If you think you are a bad writer, writing a book will make you a better writer in the process. You also learn a lot about the topic in the process because to write a book, you need to know enough. Even as I was writing this book, I had to do lots of research.

912. Go geocaching. Geocaching is an outdoor treasure hunting game. Participants are provided with GPS coordinates and must find the hidden container filled with toys and trinkets at the specific coordinates. Many people who have done geocaching say that it is a real-world adventure, it is an opportunity to get outdoors, and it took them to places they have never been to before. Aside from the gas money you pay to get there, geocaching is free.

913. Listen to audiobooks. Audiobooks are great for slow readers and they also teach people how to pronounce every word. Audiobooks are portable: listen to them in the car, while walking the dog, running, working out at the gym, painting the house, doing the laundry, etc. Try Audible.com for $14.95 per month (first 30 days are free).

914. Have sex with your partner. There are so many great benefits to having sex. Sex maintains your youthful looks, lowers blood pressure, eases depression, and makes you sleep better. Men who have sex at least twice a week are less likely to die from a heart attack. Women who have sex at least once a week have regular menstrual cycles. Remember to use a condom, or else you waste money on emergency contraception or worse, STD treatments.

915. Learn a foreign language. Knowing how to speak another language opens job opportunities. In Lubbock, many job listings state they prefer applicants who can speak both English and Spanish. Learning another language also helps you establish cross-cultural friendships. The biggest obstacle stopping people is not money but fear. How do you learn a new language on the cheap? Borrow books from the library, learn the top 1,000 commonly used words, take free online minicourses, use Google Translate, and read books and newspapers in your target language. Find people and start speaking the language immediately. You can find friends or join a local meetup group.

916. Attend religious service. You get to meet people in your local community while rejoicing in God. You also get to be part of a tightknit group of people who are supportive and loving. You get to pray for others, while others pray for you.

917. Attend religious text study. Whether it is Bible study, Quran study, or Torah study, just go. You learn much more about the text in-depth than you would at regular service. Some of my best memories include the times I attended weekly Bible study before the group disbanded. If it were still available today, I would attend every week.

918. Visit the botanical garden. Most public gardens have free entry or minimal admission prices. For instance, the Brooklyn Botanical Garden charges $15.00 for adult admission. However, if you go on Tuesdays anytime or enter on Saturdays from 10:00 AM to 12:00 PM, it is free.

919. Meditate. There are many benefits to meditation. Meditation increases your health, your happiness, your self-esteem, your focus, and your productivity. You become more compassionate. You start detaching yourself from the drama in your mind. You can find guided meditations online for free.

920. Take a photo of yourself every day. I was inspired to take a photo of myself every day after watching Noah Kalina's and Beckie Jane Brown's timelapse video on YouTube. I think it is so cool to see your face aging over a period of five years. Technology changes so fast nowadays so I won't name any particular app. Check out the Appstore on your smartphone to find the latest, most popular app for taking daily selfies with guidelines to give you the perfect alignment for timelapse videos.

921. Write a journal entry. Journals give you clarity on your thoughts and feelings, help you solve problems, and provide insight. Every time I faced a major life decision, such as deciding on my career or whether I should quit my soul-sucking job, I wrote in a journal. Buy a journal with an attractive design that you like and get started today.

922. Take a hot bubble bath. I know I wrote earlier that you should take showers instead of baths to save money on water. However, taking baths occasionally is good for relaxation.

923. Declutter. Decluttering can clear your mind and remove distractions. Less clutter means you'll find lost or misplaced items faster. Go through every room in your house. Try to do only one room per day to avoid mental exhaustion. Then take all your possessions to one part of the room and go through every single item. For every item, ask yourself these two questions: 1) do I still use it, and 2) do I love it? Then place the item in the appropriate pile for selling, donating, keeping, or trashing.

924. Have a garage sale. Garage sales help you get rid of things you no longer need while making some extra money. By selling your unwanted items, you'll have more space in your home for things you do love.

925. Donate items to charity. If you cannot sell an item, then donate it to a local charity. Lots of places will take your gently worn clothes. I usually donate to Goodwill or Salvation Army.

926. Learn magic tricks. Why should you learn magic tricks? Because you might attract your special someone the next time you do a card trick. When I first met my husband, I saw him do magic tricks with my pastor's son. I was very impressed.

927. Ride your bike. Back when I lived in New York City, I liked to bike along the Coney Island Boardwalk and along the Shore Parkway Greenway. I loved seeing the luscious ocean waves on a clear, sunny day. There is also a fresh seaside smell that cannot be had when you bike along normal roads.

928. Join a book club. By joining book clubs, you read books you otherwise would not have read and discuss what you read. You also get to meet interesting and intelligent people.

929. Plan for next year's vacation. You should plan for vacations ahead of time to get the best prices. You have more options in terms of airfare, hotels, and upgrades. Also, by planning early, you know how much money to save from each paycheck for the vacation.

930. Attend a Meetup.com event. It is free to join and attend events, but it costs money to start your own Meetup group. Depending on where you live, Meetup can be huge or be nonexistent. In New York City, there are hundreds of Meetup events to choose from. In Lubbock, there are only three active groups. At a Meetup event in New York City, I met a man named Carlos, ended up attending his birthday party, and met his friend Rod. Rod went to back to Mexico, his home country. I visited Rod in Mexico a few months ago. You never know who you will meet through Meetup.

931. Read the news. I admit that I almost never read the news. My husband reads the news every day, though. He is so well informed and has such a wide scope of knowledge. He impresses me often when we're having a discussion and he talks about something he read on the news. His news reading habit helped me many times; I use his examples when teaching personal finance.

932. Soak in a Jacuzzi. Buying and maintaining a Jacuzzi is expensive. You can save money and soak in a Jacuzzi by booking a hotel room that has one, renting an apartment with an outdoor Jacuzzi, or having a recreation center membership. I have done all three.

933. Take a group dance class. Dance classes are inexpensive. You can dance at home, but dancing at a studio gives you the opportunity to meet new people while doing a cardio workout. I used to think group dance classes were expensive until I signed up for one. I took pole-dancing classes at a studio that offered discounted morning classes for $12.00. Ballroom dancing classes were $10.00 each and Zumba classes were $15.00 each. Sometimes gyms include dance classes in the membership fee.

934. Pick fruit at an orchard. Look for a strawberry patch, an apple orchard, or grape vineyard around your town. If you live in an urban city, you need to drive out of town. Generally, it is free to visit and eat fruit at the orchard. It costs money to bring fruit back. I do recommend you buy some fruit, though. You can buy a bag of apples for $25.00. My mom told me that her friends went to an apple orchard, ate a bunch of apples, and left without buying any apples. There is frugal and then there is plain old cheap. Do not be cheap. Those farmers worked hard to grow the apples and they deserve to make a bit of money.

935. Play a musical instrument. Playing a musical instrument improves memory, develops discipline and perseverance, builds confidence, and fosters creativity. Private lessons are expensive, though. Many musicians are self-taught. My roommate is a self-taught pianist and my husband is a self-taught opera singer. You need enough interest and passion to keep learning and practicing. After a few years, you hit a ceiling, and you need to pay for private instruction. If you love it, then pay for it.

936. Take advantage of student discounts. For a list of 100 stores that give student discounts, visit BestCollegesOnline.com. The list includes school supplies, bookstores, clothing and general merchandise, electronics and digital services, food and dining, services, travel, entertainment, and transportation. The great thing about looking young is that sometimes you do not even have to show your student ID. When I was buying movie tickets for *Beauty and the Beast*, I got the student discount without even showing my ID. The only drawback to looking young is that you can look too young. One time, a cop stopped me on the sidewalk and asked for my ID. She thought I was committing truancy. I didn't know whether to be flattered or upset that the cop thought I was 16 years old when I was 21.

937. Contribute to an open-source project. This one is for IT people. Open source means the source code is open for any developer to download, examine, and improve upon. Developers are motivated to contribute to open-source projects for various reasons. Some do it to gain experience and build a resume. Many think it is a form of giving back because they themselves use open-source software.

938. Exercise. I love exercising, but I hate going to the gym. The first thing that comes to mind when you tell someone to exercise is weight training. Exercise is much more than that. There are many exercises you can do: aerobic, barre, bodyweight, Cross-Fit, cycling, dance, gymnastics, high-intensity interval training, hiking, hydrotherapy, judo, Pilates, rock climbing, rowing, running, sports, taekwondo, tai chi, twirling, walking, wrestling, yoga, etc. Try several to find what you like.

939. Play sports. Like exercise, you are not limited to America's favorite sports: football, basketball, and baseball. For a complete list of sports from around the world, visit TopEndSports.com. I highly recommend you check it out and see whether anything interests you.

940. Turn on the water sprinkler. If you have kids, play in the sprinkler with your kids. It's lots of fun!

941. Cook your meals in advance. People dislike cooking because it is time-consuming. It is easy to eat at restaurants or buy convenience foods, but it is unhealthy and wastes a lot of money. Set aside a few hours on the weekend to cook a batch of your meals ahead of time. Store it in Tupperware with a label that states the contents and the date and then put it in the freezer. Defrost and reheat when you are ready to eat.

942. Make a time capsule. You will need a retrieval date, a location, a container, a letter to the future, and objects to go into the time capsule. The best objects are ones that represent present life. You can include popular toys or tools, labels or packaging of favorite foods or other products (including price tags), newspapers, magazines, photographs, journals, letters, currency, your favorite things, clothes, and current technology.

943. Open a time capsule. Once the retrieval date has arrived, open the time capsule.

944. Soak your feet in a foot spa bath massager at home. Buy one on Amazon and check the reviews before you buy. The medium quality massagers are in the $50.00 range. I think this is a good investment, especially if you work a job where you stand on your feet all day. Do this instead of going to the spa.

Chapter 26

Travel

Cheap Vacations

945. Have a staycation. I know people who do not use their vacation days because they do not like to travel. If that's the case, have a staycation instead. Use your vacation days, please! You can relax at home if you like. Catch up on activities you put off for the past year. Explore your own city, town, or state.

946. Spend a night with your partner at a local bed and breakfast. Both of you get to relax without paying too much money. A local bed and breakfast in my area costs $104.00 per night—maximum.

Overland Travel

947. Go on a cheap road trip. Road trips can be cheap if you plan well. Always make a budget. Find inexpensive lodging and bring a water cooler full of semi-perishable foods.

948. Carpool on road trips. Split the cost of gas, tolls, lodging, and grocery food among your friends. The wrong way to do this is to make someone pay for gas this time and then make someone else pay next time. It will never be even and people who end up paying more become grumpy and resentful. The right way to do this is to pool expenses before the trip begins. For example, everyone contributes $100.00 into an envelope for gas and lodging. When the money runs out, everyone contributes to the pool again. At the end of the trip, divide the remaining money evenly.

949. Use GasBuddies.com for road trips. Input your location, destination, and vehicle information on the site's trip cost calculator. The software finds the cheapest gas stations along your road trip route.

950. Travel by bus. It is slower and cheaper. Wanderu.com compares ticket prices from all bus companies in the United States.

951. Travel by Amtrak. Depending on the distance and where you are going, sometimes it is cheaper to travel by Amtrak instead of by plane. Know your options and compare. If Amtrak were cheaper, I would go for it. One time, I took the Amtrak from New York City to Fort Lauderdale. It was cheaper and I loved it for more reasons than just money. Why? Because unlike going by plane, I don't need to arrive at the train terminal three hours before departure. Because I hate going through the TSA security check every time I need to board a plane. Because I avoid all the long lines. Because there are no assigned seats on Amtrak, so I do not feel like a second-class citizen. Because I can look out the window and see beautiful scenery instead of white clouds.

952. Travel by walking. It takes 20 million steps and several years of determination to walk around the world. Walking is free.

Air Travel

953. Travel internationally. Sometimes it is cheaper to travel domestically, but sometimes it is cheaper to travel internationally depending on the country. I know this sounds preposterous. Think about it, though. It might be cheaper to travel to South America or Southeast Asia than to California. The cost of living in California is extremely high compared to other places, and it is also a popular destination, so ticket prices are higher to reflect the demand. It is possible to buy a roundtrip ticket from the USA to Colombia for only $366.00, which is extremely cheap. When you get there, you also pay less because of the lower cost of living.

954. Work for an airline as a flight attendant. Flight attendants get between 10 and 21 days off per month. As a flight attendant, you are also eligible for free flights, along with discounts for hotels, car rentals, other airlines' flights, and vacation packages.

955. Encourage a family member to work for an airline. I have a friend named Robert who travels internationally on a regular basis. I wondered how Robert managed to get all this money to pay for airfare. It turns out that Robert's daughter works as an engineer for United Continental Airlines. Because of that, he is eligible for free flights. The only thing is, he must be on standby. If he is already at the airport and the flight turns out to be full, he waits for a different flight to a different destination. Once he gets the "okay," he runs across the terminal to catch the flight. He never knows where he will end up going, and I guess that is part of the adventure.

956. Be flexible about where and when you want to go on vacation. I like to use SkyScanner.com because it shows the cheapest prices if you are flexible. For example, if you are flexible in terms of the destination, it shows you the cheapest plane tickets from your current location to every single country in the world. If you are flexible in terms of time, it shows you the cheapest month of the year to fly to that destination. SkyScanner.com saves me a lot of time from doing the research myself.

957. Purchase your flight tickets 54 days before departure. This is based on an article written on CheapAir.com. Do not buy your plane tickets too early or too late. Try your best to buy plane tickets between 104 and 29 days before departure. This is the prime booking window, the period when the average fare is within $10.00 of the lowest fare possible. Once you are within 14 days of departure, the ticket prices increase dramatically.

958. Compare prices between roundtrip flights and one-way flights. Sometimes roundtrip tickets are cheaper than one-way tickets. Sometimes two one-way tickets combined are cheaper than roundtrip tickets. This sounds weird, but it happens. Know your options, compare, and strategize accordingly.

959. Choose connecting flights. Nonstop flights are flights between two airports with no stops. They are the fastest way to get to your destination, but also the most expensive. With connecting flights, you'll have to take at least two different planes to get to your destination. They are inconvenient but lower in price.

960. Fly when no one wants to. Whenever something bad happens in a country (e.g., epidemics, natural disasters, terrorist attacks, war, etc.), the plane ticket prices decrease dramatically. It is the law of supply and demand; no one wants to visit that country. If you are willing to take risks, then go. Every time my friend Bob traveled to a foreign country, he always happened to be there during some disaster or battle. He survived… but then again, he's Bob.

961. Depart from major airline hubs. TravelMiles101.com has a list of major airline hubs in the United States. Departing from a major airline hub could save you hundreds of dollars. For instance, my husband wanted to go from Lubbock, TX to Oakland, CA. The plane ticket price was $426.00. If he flew from Dallas, TX instead, it would cost $197.00. To get to Dallas, he could either pay $75.00 for a roundtrip Greyhound bus ticket or drive there himself for $38.00. Either way, he would save between $154.00 and $191.00 by departing from Dallas.

962. Compare prices when changing flights. United, American, and Delta charge $200.00 to change flights. This fee is outrageously high, considering the fee is almost as high as the original fare. I had a roundtrip ticket with United Airlines to fly from Lubbock, TX to New York City. I wanted to change my departure date. United Airlines wanted me to pay $200.00 for the change fee, plus $137.00 for the ticket price difference. The total was $337.00. Meanwhile, I could buy a one-way ticket for the same exact flight for $310.00 via Google Flights. Of course, I bought it for $310.00. Shame on you, United, for charging such high fees to change a flight.

963. Do not fly United Airlines. I always flew American Airlines, but when I moved across the country from New York City to Lubbock, I flew United Airlines. Before moving, I closed my bank account, so I could open a new one in Texas. I only had cash on me—no debit card or credit card whatsoever. Unfortunately, United Airlines charged $7.99 for inflight entertainment and only accepted card payments. I never knew that because I always flew American Airlines, which offers inflight entertainment for free! I hate United Airlines for many reasons, and this is just one more reason.

964. Fly Southwest or Alaska Airlines. Southwest does not charge a change fee. If you make a change within 60 days of your flight, Alaska Airlines does not charge a change or cancellation fee.

965. Travel light. Airlines in America like to nickel and dime you for everything, especially when it comes to baggage fees. Many international airlines offer your first checked bag for free, but not in America. In America, expect to pay $25.00 for your first checked bag and $35.00 for a second checked bag. The only domestic airline that offers first and second checked bags for free is Southwest. (Go Southwest!) I like to travel with only one carryon bag to avoid all checked baggage fees. Check out One-Bag.com for a guide on how to travel light.

966. Do not go over the weight limit for each checked bag. Let's say you do need to check bags in. Your bag weighs 52 pounds, but the weight limit is 50 pounds. United Airlines and other domestic airlines charge $200.00 for each overweight bag. Cathay Pacific, Korean Airlines, and China Airlines never have issues whatsoever when one of your bags is a pound over. Ridiculous, right? Here we go again with domestic airlines trying to nickel and dime you for every little thing. The solution to this is simple. Take two pounds of objects out of your bag and transfer them to your carryon bag. If you are checking in two bags and one is overweight, then just distribute the weight more evenly.

967. Bring an empty water bottle to the airport. You cannot bring any liquids past security, but you can bring an empty bottle. Fill your water bottle at a water fountain after getting past security. I always did this, so I had no idea how much a bottle of water costs at the airport. I found out at Puerto Vallarta International Airport in Mexico. I had my empty bottle but couldn't find a water fountain anywhere. In Mexico, no one drinks tap water; everyone drinks bottled water. I wanted to buy a bottle of water, but as it turned out, it cost $80.00 MXN! I could buy the same thing at an OXXO convenience store for $14.50 MXN. The airport charged more than five times the regular price. What a rip-off!

968. Bring your own snacks and neck pillow to the airport. I like to pack fresh fruit, sunflower seeds, and crackers. Airport food and merchandise are expensive because you're pretty much held captive once you're at the airport. Since you have few options, retailers can charge higher prices. I once saw prepacked salads being sold for $13.99 USD! Forget about it!

Accommodation

969. Take an overnight bus or train. You save money on accommodation for one night, but you might not sleep well. Make your overnight trip a bit more comfortable by bringing a high-quality neck pillow, a blanket, a long sleeve shirt and a long pair of pants for when the temperature drops, a sleep mask, earplugs, and snacks. I did this many times before. Believe me when I tell you that these items make all the difference.

970. Use Airbnb.com. When I visited Washington, D.C., I used Airbnb for the first time. I chose the cheapest room I could find. Cheaper places often tend to be further away from the downtown area, but I did not care. If it was accessible by public transportation, it was okay. I got a place for $11.00 per night. Not bad!

971. Use Couchsurfing.com. Couchsurfing is free. The only condition is you must provide a place for guests to stay in return. (If you are female, I recommend only hosting female guests. I had an encounter where a male guest wanted to jump into my bed at 2:00 AM.) I like Couchsurfing more than using Airbnb. I had a blast every single time I used Couchsurfing while traveling. The hosts were extremely kind, shared with me their own travel stories, and showed me around their city. Traveling is much more fun when you get to stay and interact with locals.

972. Stay in hostels when traveling overseas. When you stay in a hostel, you book a bed for a night, not a room. The drawback is that hostels lack privacy because you must share the room and the bathrooms are dorm-style. Hostels are inexpensive—one night at a hostel could cost as low as $10.00 USD in some countries.

973. Ask friends or family members who work at hotels to get you an employee discount. This will work if it is a hotel franchise. It might even work if it is a local hotel. For example, I used to work at the Overton Hotel in Lubbock, TX. I thought the Overton Hotel was a small business. Then in the new employee orientation, I found out that the Overton Hotel was 1 of 15 other hotels owned by a large corporation. Every hotel had a unique name to reflect the community it was in. As an employee, my friends, family, and I were eligible for 20 percent discounts at any of the 15 hotels.

974. Bid your own price. Priceline.com has a Name Your Own Price (NYOP) feature for flights, hotels, and car rentals. Many people on TripAdvisor recommend using the NYOP feature for hotels and car rentals only, not flights. Many people complained about being charged for the wrong dates or the wrong quantity of people. Double check your dates and number of people before paying. Also, read forums on BetterBidding.com for more advice on using Priceline's NYOP.

975. Switch hotels mid-stay. The first night I landed in Puerto Vallarta, I thought my friend Rod would pick me up from the airport and let me stay at his home. Well, he was out of town, so he did not pick me up. I had no place to stay. Rod recommended me to stay at Hotel Rio Malecon. When I got there, the only rooms remaining cost $70.79 USD per night. I had to pay or else I would be homeless for the night. The next day, I checked out and walked across town with my suitcase, so I could stay at Hotel Casa Del Parque for only $39.65 per night.

Car Service

976. Ask a friend or family member to drive you to and from the airport. In New York City, my mom always drives me to and from the airport. I save $35.00 + tips by not using car service.

977. Use car service instead of parking your car at the airport. When I was at Lubbock Preston Smith International Airport, I asked the travelers around me how they got to the airport. They told me that they drove themselves to the airport and parked their car for $12.00 per day while they were away. That means that if you are away for 14 days, you pay $168.00. If that is the case, just use Uber or Lyft to get to the airport. I pay $13.00 per ride to and from the airport. It is pricey, but it is still cheaper than leaving your car parked at the airport.

978. Walk further away from the airport to catch a taxi, if possible. When Rod could not pick me up from the airport in Puerto Vallarta, I had to take a taxi to the hotel. The lady at the airport charged me $360.00 MXN. A few days later, I needed to go to the bus station but arrived at the airport by accident. I freaked out because taxi fares were so expensive. Apparently, taxi drivers at the airport were part of a union. They would have charged me at least $200.00 MXN. A local instructed me to walk outside of the airport, cross the footbridge, and catch a cab on the other side. They charged me $80.00 MXN.

979. Avoid renting a car at the airport. Local car rental agencies offer lower prices. By going local, you also avoid paying extra surcharges that airport-based car rental agencies often charge.

During Your Travels

980. Travel like a local. If possible, avoid all the touristy areas and try to eat at restaurants that locals would eat at. When I went to Puerto Vallarta in Mexico, I didn't feel comfortable exploring outside of the touristy areas. One night, I spent $180.00 MXN for a burrito at a touristy restaurant. A few days later, in Torreon, I finally met up with my Mexican friends Rod and Michelle. They took me to a local restaurant, and I found out burritos only cost $22.00 MXN. I wanted to shoot myself in the foot for paying eight times the normal price.

981. Do not buy souvenirs or trinkets. I never buy tacky knick-knacks or meaningless trinkets to bring home for friends and family. I think the experience matters more than buying overpriced souvenirs that can't even fit into my already full suit-case. In lieu of buying souvenirs, have the time of your life and take lots of pictures. Tell your friends and family that you didn't buy any souvenirs because you would rather them have the same amazing experience you did. Encourage them to experience it for themselves.

982. Fill your suitcase with old clothes if you want to buy things on your trip. If you still want to buy souvenirs or trinkets or new clothes on your trip, consider packing old clothes. Toward the end of your trip, discard your old clothes. By doing this, you can keep one suitcase and still have space for new possessions. You avoid paying oversized or overweight baggage fees this way.

983. Use a Charles Schwab Visa Platinum Debit Card when traveling internationally. I love this card. There are many reasons why you should use this card when traveling. First, Charles Schwab requires no minimum deposit to open and charg-es no maintenance fees at all. That means the card is completely free. Second, you can use the card abroad without paying any cur-rency conversion fees for debit card transactions. Third, when you withdraw cash from an ATM, you get the local currency at the exchange rate of the day. Finally, the best thing about this card is that there are no ATM fees worldwide! My friend Romina told me that when traveling, she uses a credit card that charges annual fees and foreign transaction fees. Why pay more when you don't have to? Just use a Charles Schwab Visa Platinum Debit Card.

Chapter 27

Debt

Managing Debt

984. Never get into debt in the first place. If you have no debt, then great. You save thousands of dollars by not paying interest to banks. Most people never get ahead financially because of debt.

985. Pay off all your debts and never get into debt again. Keep your eyes on the goal. Take a sheet of paper and write down the total amount you owe. Hang this sheet of paper somewhere visible to remind you of your goal. Update the number every month.

986. Make your debt payments on time every month. Plan by setting a budget and knowing when your debt payments are due. For example, your credit card payment is due on May 17, and you get a paycheck on May 15 and May 30. Budget the May 15 paycheck to make your credit card payment. Quit wasting money on expensive late fees that range from $15.00 to $35.00.

987. Make more than the minimum payment. Look at your statement to see how much of your payment goes toward interest. When you make a minimum payment, most of the payment goes toward interest instead of the principal balance. You'll find that out of a $35.00 minimum payment, $31.00 goes toward interest and $4.00 goes toward the balance. At that rate, you waste so much money by paying interest while barely paying off your debt.

988. Pay off debt using the avalanche method. Under the debt avalanche method, you pay off the debt with the highest interest rate first. Pretend you owe money on a credit card, student loan, and auto loan. The credit card charges 15.07% APR, the student loan charges 4.29% APR, and the auto loan charges 4.79% APR. Focus all your attention on paying off the credit card while making minimum payments on the other debts. Once the credit card is paid off, focus all your attention on paying off the auto loan. Once that is paid off, focus all your attention on paying off the student loan. Sure, your interest accumulates when you make minimum payments. But since you're paying interest anyway, you might as well pay less interest.

989. Pay off debt using the snowball method if the avalanche method is too overwhelming. If you feel overwhelmed, then pay off your debt using the snowball method. I truly believe with all my heart that this is the fastest method to paying off your debt. Check out the YouTube video, "The Debt Snowball," by Countryside Christian Center. I think the video explained it much better than I ever could.

990. Liquidate big-ticket items to lower your debt. If you just bought something expensive (e.g., car, hot tub, mattress, furniture, etc.), sell it for the highest resale value you can get. Avoid pawn shops, as you won't get much money. It sucks, I know, but I'm being honest with you. If you want to buy something expensive, pay in full at the point of sale instead of getting into more debt. Quit paying unnecessary interest.

Credit Cards

991. Pay your credit card balance in full every month. People think I hate credit cards, but I do approve of them when people pay their balance in full every month. This is obvious, yet 65 percent of Americans do not pay their balance in full every month. If you keep a running balance every month, then you waste money by paying interest. Any interest you pay cancels out any cash back or travel rewards you get.

992. Negotiate with credit card companies to lower your interest rate. At a financial seminar that I taught, a student named John tried this. John was 80 years old and owed money on a few credit cards with 25% APR. He called customer service, told the representative that he was 80 years old and didn't know how much longer he had to live. He wanted to pay off his debts before dying, but with such a high interest rate and minimum payment due every month, he could never pay off debts. Do you know what happened? He lowered his interest rate down to 0% for all his credit cards. He even lowered his minimum monthly payments down to zero, so long as he paid all his debts back within the next three years. John planned to pay off his debts in much less than three years. Everyone in the class was so happy to hear this great news.

993. Transfer your credit card balance to a new card with 0% interest. Make sure the balance transfer fee is lower than the amount of money you save on the reduced interest. This damages your short-term credit, but it doesn't matter if you never plan on getting into debt again.

994. Cut your credit cards. That way, you pay down your credit card debt without accumulating more in the process.

995. Freeze your credit cards in a block of ice. If you don't have the courage to cut your credit cards, then do this instead. Your credit card is still there for moments when you need it, but you must wait for the ice to thaw before you can spend. You have a few hours to see whether your spending urge is still there.

996. Put your credit cards in a lock box. Lock your cards up and give the key to someone you trust. Make sure that the person is not an enabler for your spending addiction.

Student Loans

997. Begin paying student loans in your freshman year. Too many college students wait until after the postgraduation grace period is over. In fact, most do not even know their student loan balance when they are still in school. If you start paying before you graduate, then your balance will be lower by the time interest starts accumulating. In the long-term, you pay less in interest.

998. Avoid consolidating your student loans. Student loan consolidation reduces your monthly payments, but there is a big drawback. You end up paying thousands of dollars in interest over the life of the loan.

999. Consolidate your student loans if you must, but only the high interest ones. If you must consolidate, then do it when you can get a lower interest rate and only for the high interest loans. Make sure you get a fixed interest rate, not a variable interest rate. Variable interest rates look appealingly low, but they always increase after a few years.

1000. Avoid income-based repayment plans for your student loans. These federal programs make monthly payments affordable and manageable. However, in the long term, the monthly payments do not cover the monthly interest. The interest accumulates and borrowers end up with a larger balance than before. The federal government says the balance will be forgiven after 25 years, but do you believe it? So much can change in the next 25 years. There is no guarantee that student loan forgiveness will still be available.

My Final Tip

1001. Hire me. Most people have the information at their fingertips. They know how to save money and pay off debt, but they do not actually do it. It's like trying to lose weight. Everyone knows they must eat less and exercise more. How many people succeed? The first person I ever taught paid off $9,897.00 in debt in three months. Contact me. I can help you achieve the financial results you want.

Bibliography

Blickenstaff, E. (2020, March 13). *Homemade Baby Wipes*. Retrieved from Favorite Family Recipes: https://www.favfamilyrecipes.com/homemadebabywipesrecipe/

Blyskal, J. (2018, October 24). *Is pet insurance worth it?* Retrieved from The Washington Post: https://www.washingtonpost.com/lifestyle/home/ispetinsuranceworthit/2018/10/23/64ff3dfaccb111e8a3e644daa3d35ede_story.html

Edelman, R. (2016, January 15). *Why So Many Lottery Winners Go Broke*. Retrieved from Fortune: https://fortune.com/2016/01/15/powerballlotterywinners/

EnergySage. (2021, July 8). *Energy Conservation: 10 Ways to Save Energy*. Retrieved from EnergySage: https://www.energysage.com/energyefficiency/101/waystosaveenergy/

Haspel, T. (2020, January 27). *Most dietary supplements don't do anything. Why do we spend $35 billion a year on them?* Retrieved from The Washington Post: https://www.washingtonpost.com/lifestyle/food/mostdietarysupplementsdontdoanythingwhydowespend35billionayearonthem/2020/01/24/947d29703d6211eabacaeb7ace0a3455_story.html

Hurd, E., & Konsko, L. (2020, July 27). *Credit Cards Can Make You Spend More, but It's Not the Full Story.* Retrieved from NerdWallet:
https://www.nerdwallet.com/article/creditcards/creditcards makeyouspendmore

Imbens, G. W., Rubin, D. B., & Sacerdote, B. I. (2001, September). Estimating the Effect of Unearned Income on Labor Earnings, Savings, and Consumption: Evidence from a Survey of Lottery Players. American Economic Review, 91(4), 778794. Retrieved from
https://www.aeaweb.org/articles?id=10.1257/aer.91.4.778

Jacobs, T. (2017, June 14). *How to Bolster Your Willpower at the Supermarket.* Retrieved from Pacific Standard:
https://psmag.com/economics/howtobolsteryourwillpowerat thesupermarket33562

Livingston, G., & Cohn, D. (2010, June 25). *Childlessness Up Among All Women; Down Among Women with Advanced Degrees.* Retrieved from Pew Research Center:
https://www.pewresearch.org/socialtrends/2010/06/25/chil dlessnessupamongallwomendownamongwomenwithadvanceddegrees/

Molina, B. (2019, April 9). *Vitamin, mineral supplements don't lower risk of early death: Study.* Retrieved from USA TODAY:
https://www.usatoday.com/story/news/health/2019/04/09 /vitaminmineralsupplementsdontlowerriskearlydeathstudy/34 08637002/

Moore, S. (n.d.). *Rebate Madness How to Avoid the Rebate Trap.* Retrieved from ConsumerAffairs:
https://www.consumeraffairs.com/consumerism/rebate_ma dness01.html

Norton, M. P. (2018, August 27). *Survey: Fresh Produce Cheaper At Mass. Farmers Markets Than Supermarkets.* Retrieved from WBUR News: https://www.wbur.org/news/2018/08/27/surveyfreshprodu cecheaperatmassfarmersmarketsthansupermarkets

Ostroski, J. (2021, January 11). *Fewer Than 4 In 10 Americans Could Pay A Surprise $1,000 Expense From Savings, Survey Finds.* Retrieved from Bankrate: https://www.bankrate.com/banking/savings/financialsecurit yjanuary2021/

Taylor, C. (2015, June 17). *70% of Rich Families Lose Their Wealth by the Second Generation.* Retrieved from Time: https://time.com/3925308/richfamilieslosewealth/

Tuttle, B. (2011, July 20). *Study: Why You Should Shop for Groceries with a Cart, Not a Basket.* Retrieved from TIME: https://business.time.com/2011/07/20/studywhyyoushoulds hopforgrocerieswithacartnotabasket/

U.S. National Library of Medicine. (2020, September 21). *Storing your medicines: MedlinePlus Medical Encyclopedia.* Retrieved from MedlinePlus: https://medlineplus.gov/ency/patientinstructions/000534.ht m

University of Chicago Press Journals. (2009, March 31). *Buyer Beware: Touching Something In A Store Increases Perceived Ownership.* Retrieved from ScienceDaily: www.sciencedaily.com/releases/2009/03/090331112723.htm

Share Your Thoughts: Leave a Review

Your Opinion Matters! I would truly appreciate hearing your thoughts about my book. In the world of book publishing, honest reviews from diverse readers hold immense value. By sharing your review, you'll help prospective readers determine if this book is right for them. Additionally, your valuable feedback will boost the visibility of my book and enable me to reach a broader audience.

Please go to AnnieMargaritaYang.com/save-review to share your re-view, and thank you for your support!

About The Author

Annie Margarita Yang is the go-to finance guru for Millennials refusing to lose in a system stacked against them. A candid, no-fluff YouTube personality and best-selling author of *1,001 Ways to Save Money* and *The 5-Day Job Search*, Annie is a part of the group she educates—the demographic most misunderstood because they must overcome finance challenges previous generations didn't.

She is skilled at creating easy-to-follow money-saving systems, intentional in addressing the unique concerns of Millennials, and relentless about creating financial independence.

With more than 1 million views on YouTube, her witty approach to tough talk sets her apart from others.

An accountant by trade but most passionate about personal finance, Annie dodged student loan debt by leaping into the world of minimum wage jobs after high school. She grew a love for frugal living, self-education, and planning for the future during those years. Annie understood that while it wasn't easy to avoid debt, it was possible. She later earned her B.A. in Communications from Thomas Edison State University.

By day, Annie works as an accounting manager and business operations leader in the real estate industry. By night, she gives her all to help others overcome the biggest obstacle of their lives. She specializes in saving money and helping people free up funds in their budgets for the things that truly matter in life.

Annie lives with her husband in Boston, where she is fully committed to learning the piano!

Also By The Author

The 5-Day Job Search: Proven Strategies To Answering Tough Interview Questions & Getting Multiple Job Offers

Unlock the secret to landing your dream job in just five days! Finance expert Annie Margarita Yang introduces her groundbreaking system, *The 5-Day Job Search*, transforming your job-seeking experience.

This versatile guide caters to job hunters across industries, ensuring multiple job offers even during economic downturns.

Experience incredible benefits, such as:
- An easy-to-follow formula
- Finding a fulfilling career
- Joining a top company with a perfect work culture fit
- Rapid responses from companies
- Mastering the art of selling yourself
- Acing interviews with confidence, leading to written job offers 90% of the time
- Securing a job with a significant raise

Join satisfied readers who have transformed their careers with *The 5-Day Job Search*.

Get your copy of *The 5-Day Job Search* today!

AnnieMargaritaYang.com